THE AUTHORITY
PLAYBOOK

THE AUTHORITY PLAYBOOK

BY DILLON KIVO

AUTHORITY
TITANS PUBLISHING
www.authoritytitans.com

Table of Contents

Foreword

Personal Branding is a crucial part of your identity. The things you first see when you Google yourself will be the first impression people will have of who YOU truly ARE! With the presence of social media nowadays, people can already view your day-to-day activities and possibly, can already make some assumptions about you—whether it would be to your expediency or disadvantage. The main goal is to act in control of the information they find and have legitimate sources back you up — which is the news. People end up believing a more credible source and halt from making unnecessary conjectures about how you do what you do.

Getting the help you need to attain an effective personal brand can be tough, but it doesn't have to feel like an uphill battle. Dillon Kivo is an expert when it comes to success and influence, having helped high profile business people achieve their goals like myself.

His ability to get clients' news coverage solid across all mediums is nothing short of amazing. I've watched Dillon repeatedly get clients into mainstream press and onto Television and if you check out his Instagram @dillonkivo, you'll see that he's also been featured over and over across major news outlets & media publications. He's done it for himself, me, and many others. There's even a huge chance that you have already encountered an Authority before that DILLON KIVO has taken care of and nurtured.

So, if you want to be an authority in your niche, there's never been a better time.

This book will help you understand how to actually make it happen.

DAN FLEYSHMAN

Founder of Model Citizen Fund

Dan is the youngest founder of a publicly traded company in history. After licensing his apparel for $9.5 million dollars at the age of 19, he went on to scale the energy drink products into 55,000 retail stores.

Introduction

In the age of information, authority is key. I've worked with brands and individuals throughout my career to help them establish impactful and long-lasting authority—one that creates a legacy of success in their careers and life. Because of this growth, they have obtained wealth, influence, and, ultimately, a freedom that they had never thought was possible.

The driving force of your success is your ability to establish yourself as trustworthy. If you are not viewed as trustworthy, no one will listen to you, regardless of knowledge. As an authority, you can charge more, gain more influence, and live a life you never imagined. Throughout this book, I will teach you how to develop authority and change the trajectory of your future.

If you've read my book, *Authority Titans*, then you are probably familiar with the concept of being an authority in your industry.

There is no greater force for success in the world. It separates the experts from the novices and the influencers from the followers. With it, you exude a strong presence among your peers, a more prominent position in your industry, and the ability to live an impactful life. This book aims to empower you and narrow your focus on those areas that will elevate you as an authority in your industry.

In addition, I will help you identify your authority, build it, and maintain it. The thing about authority is it's hardly a one-and-done matter. Like anything worth having, it requires maintenance. So, you have to daily wake up and recommit to the goal of becoming and maintaining your status as an authority in your industry. By the end of this book, you'll know exactly what it takes to be an Authority Titan, a source of infinite knowledge, skill, social proof, expertise, and experience.

You have to approach the notion of success the way good parents approach their duty to their children. It's an honor, an obligation, and a priority.

—GRANT CARDONE

CHAPTER 1

My First Job Was at McDonald's

What comes to mind when you see the word authority? While there are many types of authority, punitive authority is almost always what people think of first. This type of authority uses punishment to exercise control and establish dominance. However, that isn't the authority I speak of in this book. Instead, I want to show you how to hit that sweet spot where influence intersects expertise. I will share how to gain authority in your industry by fusing the shared core concepts of influence and expertise. Social proof, skill, knowledge, experience, and consistency are the keys to becoming a titan in your industry.

Speaking of experience, you may be wondering why you should take advice from me or implement any of what I am saying into your life. Let me try to answer it for you. First, I am the founder of several seven-figure companies. My public relations agency, Authority Titans, is on the verge of hitting eight figures in its first four years of business. I have accomplished all of this by implementing the core competencies stated above. I didn't always have the answers; I had to search for and fine-tune them. Alone, they will not achieve the desired results. Skill without social proof, knowledge without experience, or lack of consistency will kill your chances of rising to the level of being recognized as an authority in your industry.

In no way did I start at the top, or anywhere even close to the top, for that matter. I dreamed of playing hockey in the NHL. What did I do in the meantime? I worked at McDonald's. Glamourous, right? While I did get a few offers from colleges to play hockey, I had no clue what to study or what I even wanted to do after college. I decided to get realistic about my chances of playing hockey as a career. I loved the sport and was pretty good at it, but going pro wasn't going to happen. So, at twenty-one years old, I quit hockey and decided it was time to pursue a career.

Honestly, I wasn't even sure what I would do. I was living in Virginia Beach at the time. I remember as a child I thought firefighters were "pretty cool." They got to help people, and it was a respected career. So, I went through the training, and in a few months, I started my new job with the Norfolk Fire Department. It was exciting to have a job, but I quickly realized that this wasn't the job for me. The job paid me $36,800/year, and I was unhappy. I couldn't even afford to pay for a mortgage with the money I brought home. I also realized that I was a germaphobe. Working around all the blood and medical stuff started to gross me out. That's when I started asking myself a question: *How can I help people, avoid germs, and make money?*

About the same time I started asking this question, I met Paul. He was a friendly guy who owned a business and visited Virginia for a few days. We hit it off, and he asked me if I wanted to do some work for him. Happy to make extra money that didn't involve blood and touching people's nastiness, I said yes. I started doing some website work for him for $300/week and realized this was a great opportunity. I could land a few more people to work for, and I could easily make more money than I earned as a firefighter, which sounded perfect and beat what I was currently doing. I worked for him remotely for a couple of months, and I quickly became more interested in what he did. He relished life, his business was worth more than 2 billion dollars!

He was also interested in me because he told me that he was impressed with my work and offered to mentor me one day. I couldn't believe it! I told him yes, packed up all my stuff, and moved to Nashville. The next two and a half years changed my life forever. When I moved there, he made me his right hand man. I did everything for him. I Picked up his kids from school, grocery shopping, cleaned his pool and washed his Lamborghini,

Porsche, Ferrari, and Rolls Royce. In return, he paid me a fair amount of money, and I got to see how he ran his billion dollar business. It was one of the best times of my life. When I wasn't running his errands, I helped him build his businesses. I watched as he fired/hired people, helped him set up his online presence, and assisted in other areas of his business. Those two and a half years were the most exhausting but amazing years of my life. I learned everything about business during this time and from a guy that made millions of dollars every day. I can't tell you what he saw in me to this day. All I knew was that I would ensure Paul would see how hard I could work. My commitment paid off. At the end of that time, I realized that I was ready to do this independently. If I could do all of this for Paul, I definitely could do it for myself!

The rest is history. At the age of twenty-three, I stepped out on my own. In 2015, I started my agency, the Kivo Media Group. Since then, in just six years, we've gone from operating as a small business startup to securing clients in major news networks and making more money in a month than most ever make in a lifetime. I've been a contributor for Forbes and Entrepreneur Media. In addition, I have authored and co-authored several books on the subject of authority. My company's clientele consists of celebrities like Ice Cube, North Carolina Panthers, Millionaire Penny Stock Trader Tim Sykes, real estate mogul Manny Khoshbin, and many NFL, NBA, and MLB players, first publicly traded CBD company in the world cbdMD. I have worked with each of them to promote events and develop their PR Strategies. These are people I would have never even met, much less promoted and worked with, had I not made my transition from being a nobody to someone with authority. The secrets that I learned have gotten me past the hurdles many people face and have landed me in newspaper articles for absolutely free. I promise that they can do the same for you because they already have done so for many others like you.

The strategies and tricks I learned to get to this position of authority were mostly due to the things I learned while working under Paul in Virginia at that first startup job. The time I spent working at McDonald's was the worst, hands down. I was exhausted, felt ineffective, and it made me doubt myself, but it also helped me realize I wanted more and was capable of more. I certainly learned how to push through exhaustion—mental and physical. That drive led me to search for someone experienced who could teach me how to promote and position myself for success. I found a mentor to show me the process and help me understand things that had worked for him and his inner circle of connections. His coaching and advice are what ultimately made the difference for me.

When I think back on my time in Nashville, I am so grateful that I had Paul as an amazing mentor. I owe my success to his mentorship. I tell the story of my process a lot because I want people to understand where I come from and how I can help them. I have experienced a lot of seasons where I've been stagnant and a lot of seasons of exponential growth. The key difference between these times was the existence of a mentor in my life. Initially, I was working on my own, just using trial and error.

After I trained under a successful entrepreneur, I essentially skipped a whole flight of stairs on the way up. My process accelerated and became infinitely simpler. He recommended things that became part of my strategy, and I avoided what he told me to avoid. This same kind of mentorship is what I can provide you through this book. The subject we're going to tackle here is something that I had not yet mastered when I left home and moved to Virginia, the concept of becoming an authority. I'm going to mentor you from beginning to end and give you the kind of education I believe most business owners and people, in general, are lacking. By the end of this book, I want to make you an authority and show you how to remain one for years to come.

I have taught numerous entrepreneurs and athletes on the subject of authority and have been able to help them promote their businesses, brands, and personal image. That's me now. I've been able to fly private, meet with celebrities, and honestly live the absolute best life I could imagine living. As amazing as this is, none of it would be possible without first establishing myself as an authority in my industry. In the pages that follow, I will share steps with you that will develop you as an authority and build the life you never dreamed was possible.

What Is My Goal for You?

Before we get into the details of being an authority, I want to cover what this book can do for you. We will break down some ideas about entrepreneurship that have been built over time and probably influence many of the decisions you make. I was subject to many theories about myself and others around me, which kept me doubting when I first started. So many jobs and systems put in place want you to grind for twenty years so you can get enough to scrape by. Either that, or they want you to be your absolute best self as an influencer, salesperson, or spokesperson so that they can reap the benefits of your hard work. I think we can agree this structure is in almost every field on earth.

People grind harder every day for someone else to benefit from their expertise or influence. If you go on Instagram or see endorsements and ad campaigns, you'll see thousands of people with influence selling products. The concept of putting yourself out there is very much alive and well in the modern world. The saddest thing is seeing people with influence work long and hard but brushed off because they lack the expertise to establish authority, and vice versa—seeing those experts struggle because they lack the influence to obtain authority in their industry. I don't like watching people get glanced over and underestimated like I initially was. There's no reason anyone reading this book can't take what they know or can do and achieve a meaningful life from it.

I told you about my mentor Paul, a great guy to work for and an amazing mentor. I meant every word I said about him being a reliable mentor too. While working for him, I saw that it didn't matter how hard I or anyone around me worked. As long as I didn't have the connections he had or authority he carried, we were simply operating on two different levels. It wasn't like he was cheating me out of money or that I wasn't working hard enough. The truth is, I simply wasn't working smart enough until I learned how to take what I knew, combine it with who I knew and could influence, and created several businesses that I could not have even imagined running a few years before. All of this was made possible by the secrets Paul taught me, and it's those secrets that have driven my career since then.

My goal is to take you from whatever you may currently be operating as, expert or influencer, and elevate your potential by making you an authority. As an authority, you'll be able to break free from that struggle to "make it." All of the cold calling, random emails, and hard work with no direction can stop, and you can make purposeful, effective steps in the right direction. While there's a lot to be said for the hard work all of your efforts have required, I think you deserve to see them become a whole lot more effective.

My Promise

The strategies and ideas in this book have taken social media accounts and quickly accelerated them from 1,000 to 50,000 followers. They have taken relatively unknown, highly successful individuals and gotten them interviewed, written about, and published. You can trust me here because I have not only worked my way up to the point of authority, but I have also helped many others achieve this goal. It's not enough to be famous, and it's not enough to be the smartest guy in the room. What matters is establishing yourself in a position of authority. To do that, you must have the know-how. That's a simple truth. At the end of the day, it's a matter of knowing the perfect formula to establish and maintain industry authority.

These steps have achieved results time and time again. I can promise you that this process was well into the process of development long before I ever discovered it. We're going to take the strategies thousands have used to obtain authority and simplify them so they can apply to your unique situation and goals.

If you're interested in seeing how I went from McDonald's to Forbes in such a short time, then you might want to keep reading. If you also want to skip ahead and avoid decades of experience and networking to slightly advance in your field, then again, you'll want to keep reading. Give me some of your time here, and I'll save you weeks, months, and maybe even years in your pursuit of how to establish your authority. That is my promise to you.

In life, lots of people know what to do, but few people actually do what they know.
Knowing is not enough! You must take action.

—TONY ROBBINS

What Is an Authority?

AUTHORITY = consistency + social proof + skill + knowledge + experience

To teach you how to become a recognized authority, you must first understand what it means. The equation above seems simple enough. Yet, it takes a mastery of the skill set above to achieve the desired result of becoming an authority. Consistency, social proof, skill, knowledge, and expertise (elements that I will describe in detail later in this book) must all be blended precisely and executed near flawlessly, or you will miss your mark.

What Is Authority?

To define authority, we need to think about it in the context of your success. Sure, the word "authority" is easy enough to understand. Still, in the context of your authority, that word means you are an individual who commands respect and is considered a leader in your network and field. I'm not talking about some image you simply project out there. You're not faking it as an authority; you're not tricking people or using marketing tactics to pull the wool over their eyes. As an authority, what you're doing is actively promoting your skills and expertise as you grow it. You're becoming effective at delivering value to every client. You're becoming the go-to guy when FOX, CBS, or NBC wants to interview a subject or the guy your friends refer everyone to when they need help in your field. Authority opens doors that were once closed because it puts you at the center of every inner circle. You're becoming the one guy everyone talks about when they think of your industry. For example, if you need to order something online, you think of Jeff Bezos and Amazon. If you think of electric cars, you think of Elon Musk and Tesla. They are the perfect example of authorities in their industry.

As an authority, you're adding the missing pieces needed to ensure growth. Essentially, you're either adding clout to the influence you already have, or you're grabbing the attention of industry leaders for the things that you already know and do. You're doing this to make your business effective or your networks wider. I could keep going, but I think you get the idea. There is no shortage of advantages to becoming an authority.

It should be no surprise that leaders are typically an authority in their field. Leaders drive the world. Without them, the rest of the world might wonder aimlessly—without direction or purpose. All talent and skill would be left unorganized, disconnected, and unproductive if not for those who feel the pull to lead. Without leaders, innovation would be at a standstill. Leadership is especially important when establishing a brand, business, or anything you hope stands the test of time. Similar to the qualities needed to be an authority, leadership requires credibility. No one will follow a leader's orders, listen to an expert's advice, or be swayed by the influence of someone they don't trust.

An entrepreneur with authority is a person who understands the technical details of his or her business and having the foresight to envision possibilities for promotion and growth. This type of person educates him or herself to become the expert and influencer. This knowledge gathering is essential and lays the foundation for becoming an industry authority.

Did you catch the quote by Tony Robbins at the beginning of this chapter? "In life, lots of people know what to do, but few people actually do what they know. Knowing is not enough! You must take action." Robbins says that you are at your best when you do what you know and take action to make what you already know work for you. An authority does this extremely well. Elon Musk didn't build Tesla because of his knowledge—and the guy's a freaking genius! He became an authority because he took action. That is a huge piece of the puzzle. Many people are one puzzle piece away from an unending source of lifelong impact. You can have all of the knowledge or influence on earth, but without combining the two, you will never achieve the results I know you are capable of achieving. You connect the two; you'll reap the dividends for years to come.

The best part about this is that there is never a bad time to become an authority. People retire, new products come out, and there is always a shift in the market. So, while that keeps us on our toes, it also allows people to introduce themselves as an authority.

If you're not dreaming big for yourself, who's doing it for you?

-GARY VAYNERCHUK

An Authority Mindset

Often, the biggest obstacle that keeps someone from achieving authority status is him or herself. More specifically, it's our mindset. Unfortunately, we have been conditioned by our upbringing, society, or some other intangible that makes us think we aren't good enough or smart enough to be an authority. It sounds simple, but that is the difference between someone who becomes an authority and who doesn't. To figure out how to place yourself in a prepared position for success, you need to address your thoughts and opinions. Your mindset needs to be that of an authority. Not only will you need to understand how you can obtain success, but you'll also need to strengthen your mindset. Many try to accomplish great things in their lives; unfortunately, many fail. About 20 percent of all small businesses fail in the first year. By year five, that percentage shoots up to 50 percent. Half of all small businesses fail, and half of all small business owners have to clean up the mess and move on. There's no one to catch them after that fall. As a small business owner, you usually take all of the responsibility and blame for the failure of your business. It's up to you to pick up the pieces and keep marching. To deal with a devastating loss and still get back up takes resilience. Most of those business owners probably don't right back to a new business, and many probably never try again. Strengthening your mind and adjusting your mindset now will save you years of trouble in the future. The proper mindset is essential in your process of building your infinite authority.

One Second Difference

Mindset is what is going to take you to the next level. We must consider the potential in terms of what it will take for you to go from where you feel you're lacking to your best self. You can think of this as finding the difference between where you want to be and where you are now. Unfortunately, this difference is what is going to keep you from achieving your full potential in life.

The difference between a semi-pro and a professional is one second. The chances you don't take, paths you veer off, and relationships you don't cultivate could be something that takes you from being stuck as a semi-pro. You cannot discount the impact a good decision-making process will have on your life. If you're struggling with indecision, and it's dictating your choices, then you'll lose that second. Those seconds come here and there, and when they show up, you take them and advance, or you let them slip by.

What's Hindering You?

Many mental blocks may be keeping you from taking the necessary steps to becoming an authority. Before we can implement the instructions that will follow in this book, we need to remove those mental blocks and replace them with thoughts that will put you on the right path to success. My problem while growing up was the sense that I lacked knowledge. As a result, I didn't go to college, which made me less of a person for several years. Going to college would have given me the confidence to do whatever I wanted to accomplish. No matter how much I wanted to help people and become a millionaire, I didn't know how or where to look.

When I found my mentor Paul, he set me on the right path. He taught me business lessons and know-how. A quick side note, I believe a mentor is the best way to get from point A to B in a business. A mentor is the best way to get from point A to B. You are following someone's footsteps who has done what I want to do for fifteen to twenty years. He was able to show me through his experience what to do and what not to do. His teaching style was simple. He didn't have a college education either, so I could relate and understand his words. When I first started my career, my questions were simple. *How can I pay my bills?* Fifty thousand a year would make that happen for me. I didn't even know I wanted to be a business owner until I was halfway into my three years with Paul. After driving around in a $175K white Porsche 911 and people stopping to take pictures and ask how you did it for a few years, it became my new normal. I drove a 1999 green Honda Accord that I bought for less than $2000. Being next to Paul showed me what was possible and made me used to it before I even had it. He was my business compass.

Limiting Beliefs

Are your limiting beliefs hindering you? If you're like most people out there, you'd probably find limiting beliefs somewhere on the list of things that hold you back at some point in life. No matter what stage in the process they're in, limiting beliefs are present in the minds of people who are setting out to accomplish anything. Limiting beliefs don't care who you are. They are present in a middle school student, and they are present for the CEO of a billion-dollar company. Everyone has to overcome them to build an authority mindset.

The thoughts and presupposed ideas we hold are limiting beliefs. If you have an opinion or thought about the world that limits you from taking action and improving your life, that is a limiting belief. It can be anything that causes negative self-talk and typically involves some version of the word "can't."

- "I can't learn how to be more efficient."
- "I can't escape my 9–5 cycle."

- "I can't ever be successful."
- "There's no way I'm worthy of respect."

You can substitute anything after the phrase *I can't*—an indicator of a limiting belief. Also, *I'm not, I'll never*, or *There's no way on earth* are phrases you may find yourself saying or at least thinking if you have limiting beliefs. These negative opinions about yourself are the kinds of thoughts that will hold you back.

There are many reasons you may have these beliefs that could hold you back. Maybe you grew up with parents who never talked about money, so you came to not understand how it works or how to make it. Perhaps you've been fired from a job in the past, so you work extra hard to please your current employer and are afraid to venture out on your own. Events like this may be the things that can cause doubts about yourself and capabilities. When we boil it down to the bones, we realize that **fear** is behind every limiting belief. We fear failure, opinion of others, unknown, and so on. When we fear, we stop taking action.

Unfortunately, we acquire these fears at a young age. We are taught from a young age that it's not okay to stand out and be bold. As a result, people avoid situations that carry the potential of making them appear foolish. I vividly remember studying and memorizing a five-minute speech when I was six years old—better than I can spell my own. I remember my teacher, Miss Lynch, called on me to read my paper, and I turned around to face my classmates. My face turned bright red. I was so nervous that I had forgotten my name. Twenty-something years later, I look back. I didn't care about bad grades or anything. It had everything to do with what people thought of me. I wanted to be cool. In the back of my head lived the fear that if I messed up, my friends might not think I was cool. That was my limiting belief. I was fearful of what people would think of me. As I got older, I realized that I self-sabotaged myself because of my irrational fear. It took some time to get over, but I did. While writing this book, I spoke in front of a few hundred people, and I remembered my name.

Identifying the Cause

The first step in sorting out limiting beliefs is to identify them. Next, look for thoughts that cause you to hesitate at things that aren't harmful or dangerous, just difficult. Think about your internal dialogue and consider the words you feed yourself throughout the day. Then, take those negative thoughts and turn them into action phrases.

For example:

Instead of	Say
"I can't learn how to be more efficient."	"I'm going to learn how to be more efficient."
"I can't focus."	"I'm going to learn how to focus."
"I can't ever be successful."	"I will make myself successful.

| "There's no way I can be respected." | "I will work to gain respect." |

Capturing and maintaining the right mindset is a major step in gaining authority. It starts with identifying the beliefs limiting your potential and eliminating them. Your opinion of your abilities is ultimately the one that matters the most. So if you make it a priority to reclaim your authority over your thought processes, you'll have a much better chance of achieving elsewhere.

Indecisiveness

Is indecision hindering you? Indecisiveness is one of the flaws that can stand in the way of someone reaching his or her potential. The inability to overcome this obstacle can break a career or relationship and keep you from ever being an authority. Simply put, indecisiveness is a business killer.

Being indecisive could have many causes, but, ultimately, each cause will result in the same outcome. If you stay indecisive, you'll become more anxious as you go forward, become less likely to take risks, and miss out on opportunities due to the inability to commit.

You don't want to keep indecisiveness in your life. You want to be decisive and effective. You want your words to be meaningful and your actions to have positive results. If you start now and eliminate this behavior, you'll save yourself hours of lost sleep and years of lost potential in the long run.

To end your streaks of indecisiveness, you need to develop habits of decision. Learn to stay focused. There are many ways to get rid of distractions, and we're all built differently in how we deal with them. For starters, replace a bad habit with a good one. Take what you're poorly doing now, and replace it with a habit that brings positive outcomes. Give yourself a chance not just to end the bad habit but to begin a new, positive one that makes you more effective.

Practice doesn't make perfect; only perfect practice will do that. So, practice perfectly and improve those areas where you currently struggle. For example, with indecisiveness, this looks like setting a time limit on your decision-making process. You limit your options and set yourself up for success by being indecisive. Over time, this new habit of making quicker decisions will replace the old one, and you'll be able to make decisions with confidence.

This strategy is similar to how an athlete trains out a bad habit. When I was playing hockey, I didn't wait for the game and then remind myself not to make mistakes. I proactively pursued my mistakes and worked to replace them with an effective alternative. I was a hockey player for several years, and if I had poor puck handling, I would focus on developing good handling skills as a replacement habit. By replacing the negative habits

When it comes to mindset, you must be proactive. First, you have to break down the old to rebuild, which doesn't come easy—the work isn't always pretty, but if there isn't a sincere desire to change, the chances of success are low. So, if you're going to accomplish this first step, you need to take the initiative and work to improve the mindset and your approach. The best way to make this possible is to get passionate. Passion will drive you to do better and be better. If you're passionate enough, the mindset will fall in line with practice.

Passion and Knowledge

Passion is one of the strongest driving forces. Your passion will determine what you want to spend time on and do your best to achieve. You need to evaluate what you are passionate about and see what elements work well within your business plans.

I tell people to make sure they are passionate about their chosen path. When you have a passion for your profession, it's virtually impossible to hate working. When I worked at McDonald's, I showed up on time and worked hard all day but did not want to do it. I was not too fond of the smells when I left work. I hated that I was only doing something to make someone else a lot of money while I took home some of the lowest paychecks I've made. There was no way I could be passionate about that job and no way I could make a career out of it. So decide what you will do and make sure you enjoy it. You will need that passion to break through the barriers.

What takes you from "maybe" to "definitely"? Passion for what you are doing and knowledge. If you're finding you're not confident, and you're indecisive, it's possible you don't know enough about the subject you're attempting to master. I knew that I understood and would enjoy doing PR and business from an early stage of my career. I also knew that due to my education and experience, I would have a greater chance of success in this field. I've had to continue learning about new niches and information in that field, but my original goal hasn't changed. What's changed is my knowledge of my specialty.

If, in your case, you don't know much about marketing or PR, but you're working night and day to start a PR firm, you're going to find that there are a lot of things that make you feel hesitant along the way, and I guarantee you most of those things come in the form of a learning curve. It's hard enough to sit at a keyboard and grind away or chase cold calls when you know what you're doing. A learning curve adds an extra layer of difficulty to that process. This curve is where most of that insecurity and hesitancy will come from and is a good obstacle to tackle early in the process to free yourself from the hesitant mindset.

Prioritize and Move Forward

Deal with your hindrances early on. Once you've identified your weaknesses, it's important to prioritize which ones you need to begin working on first and take them on. Then, ask yourself how you'll accomplish this.

"What obstacle is hindering me the most?"

"How much time does this obstacle take from my day?"

"How much more effective and efficient could I be without this obstacle?"

After this, it's a simple process of listing them out and working on them. Again, treat your self-education process and discipline as importantly as you treat your business plan. All of the negative mindsets discussed here are fixable. You only need to regulate your response to them, evaluate which ones to work on, and then make it your goal to deal with them before they hold you back any longer.

Confidence and Self-Belief

Self-belief is the beginning of confidence. For me, a lot of my confidence stemmed from my short time as a firefighter. Going through the academy, I had to wake up at three or four in the morning. We worked and trained for twelve to fourteen hours a day for eight months straight. It was insane. I wouldn't say I liked college, but college was honestly a walk in the park compared to this. A typical day was crazy. We would spend six to eight hours studying in the classroom, work out consistently (I have never done so many push-ups and sit-ups in my life), and run up to five miles a day. Despite the strenuous schedule, I crushed it! I never doubted myself when it came to the physical side; years of hockey made that part easy, but I did surprise myself with the academic side. I had never been the best student, so I thought I would struggle. Instead, I pushed hard and was determined to be the best. The result? I found myself in the top 5 percent of the class. For me, it wasn't a result of smarts; it was my confidence. I believed I could do it and let that guide me while I studied and worked my ass off.

Do you have negative self-talk about your abilities, past, or potential? If you have ever stepped out of your comfort zone, you probably have. I don't think many people couldn't benefit from a boost in confidence, but it's not always easy to identify how to achieve confidence, especially if you're already so preoccupied with your daily grind. It is, however, something you cannot afford to ignore.

My number-one tip for you, which I have repeatedly seen work, is a simple one.

*"Find out the **why**."*

Identify what it is that is causing you to lack confidence. Maybe it's a certain subject or task. For example, perhaps you aren't comfortable with public speaking because each time you've tried a speaking engagement, you couldn't stop thinking about all the people looking at you and worried you looked strange on a stage. Maybe making phone calls stresses you out because you don't know what to say or do when asked unexpected questions. What you don't feel confident about will be different depending on who you are and your experience.

Identify the things holding you back. Then you change the narrative. Changing the narrative, in this situation, looks like taking the negative experience or feeling and turning it into something that has a positive association by taking something that causes you to feel afraid and letting it make you feel excited instead. Psychologists agree that this is a great technique to hack your fight-or-flight response to stress and use that same energy to fuel your excitement for the action you're about to undertake.

Counter your thoughts if they are holding you back. Get excited instead of stressed. When you adopt this one small practice, you will start to see a subtle but significant change in your perception of new things and your emotions.

"I am nervous about speaking here tonight"

becomes

"I am excited to be speaking here tonight."

You're not lying to yourself by reminding yourself that fear and excitement are closely related. Your brain simply tells you to kick it into gear and get work done. So let it do that, and don't let it hold you back.

Practice on Small Stuff

You must practice how to successfully implement your authority mindset. If you hope to gain authority in the coming years, you will have to deal with many issues and failings requiring your attention and mental clarity. You will find that you will need to make difficult decisions about the best possible paths to take.

When scaling my agency, I hired a marketing guy to bring us more business. He was good at what he did and brought in a huge influx of leads. I remember talking to my brother Daniel and saying, "You either need to hire more people or figure something out. There's no chance I'm turning down our ad spend. I ended up hiring my brother's best friend, Zach. It worked at first, and instead of twenty calls, we did forty calls. Then he turned up the ad spend again and had to hire a third guy. Zach called his cousin Chris who had decent sales experience and would be a great fit. Now we were taking sixty calls a day. We shot up over a few months from $20K to multiple 6 figures a month. The problem was we didn't have the infrastructure to handle everything. Our writers couldn't handle the load, and things were getting behind. Our quality started going down, and with that, our client retention decreased by 10–15 percent. Ultimately, our customer experience got too bad. It was tough, but I had to power down the ads. I realized that I needed to slow down to build the systems and resources we needed to ensure our long-term success. Yes, we lost money when I powered down the ads. Yes, I slowed down our growth, but I had to ensure we had the systems in place. I had to focus on the small things. I took the time to go and hire four operational managers, fifteen writers, and fifteen more people to make calls. Looking back, that was the best thing I could do. Having the proper system in place and taking care of the details has driven my business to places I didn't think could.

McDonald's Strategy

When practicing on the small stuff, you'll find that many things need altering and adjusting over time. The best way to approach this process is to tune in to your emotions, work through the problems, and ask if the issue will matter ten years from now. Most importantly, trust yourself and your process. Trust the work you're putting in to yield the results you are ultimately looking for.

Richard and Maurice McDonald, the founders of McDonald's, virtually started the systems that now drive every fast food restaurant worldwide. Having worked as a manager there for several years, I can tell you that their system works well for what they're accomplishing. Whatever product, service, or brand you're working on, the method you choose to deliver it will make all the difference. Your processes and decision-making will ultimately prove to be infinitely more important than the actual product or service offered.

Practice your ability to make effective decisions and tune out the self-doubt and the negative mindsets. Tune in to your emotions and learn about your decision-making process to make the necessary changes and decisions. Focus on the things that matter, and from there, trust yourself and the process.

We are all different in the way we perceive the world. We must use this understanding as a guide to our communication with others.

−TONY ROBBINS

CHAPTER 4

Influencers and Experts

Infinite authority consists of two major components: influence and expertise. While both are powerful, the ultimate authority comes when you combine them. Unfortunately, we live in a world where these two components are often kept separate, consequently keeping most people from fulfilling their true potential. In today's world, many people fall into two categories. First are the people with amazing skills and knowledge of how to market and have the confidence to put themselves out there. We call them influencers. If you scroll through TikTok, Instagram, or other social media platforms, you can probably think of a few influencers that have popped up on your feed. Then, there are the experts. These would be the people you'd call if you need your website redesigned, lead generation strategy redone, or business finances balanced. They have strong knowledge about a particular industry or niche.

You most likely fell into one of these categories when you started this process. If you consider yourself an expert, I want to teach you how to influence and be more marketable. I want you to learn how to grow your network and make the most out of the skills you possess. If you're more on the influencer side of the equation, you can learn how to use your influence to accelerate your career in a particular niche and become a resident expert. Whatever you came to this study with, your ultimate goal is to understand the strengths and weaknesses of each and decide which one you need to work more on. Developing the category that you are weaker in is how you can take your potential from being more than an expert or influencer. This development is how you will ultimately achieve authority.

Influencers

What Is an Influencer?

Influencers are certainly a big deal these days. On social media platforms, especially platforms like Instagram, thousands of people have gone from unknown to famous in a small matter of time using mostly pictures and captions. This title is not limited to the internet, however. Talk show hosts, speakers, musicians, TV personalities, and even politicians have all been considered influencers in the past. Anyone who commands a large audience of followers is an influencer. They are known for their social proof and personal brand, something we'll discuss more later.

Maybe they don't own a company brand, but they can build a brand around themselves somehow.

Simply put, an influencer is someone with the ability to generate influence and whose primary source of revenue is from promotions, affiliate marketing, and his or her social media following. Influencers can be athletes, models, YouTubers, podcasters, or anyone who has gained a significant following on social media and can sway or "influence" that following. The life of an influencer is all over the internet as he or she has to maintain a certain following or certain number of posts to maintain his or her revenue and influence.

What Do Influencers Do?

It's a popular thing these days to become an influencer. They seem to get all of the perks of a celebrity and have picture-perfect lives that we all see on their social media. They monetize something (social media) that most use to share pictures and make a living off millions of people simply scrolling down their newsfeed or for your page.

There are also many ways to be an influencer that don't necessarily involve social media. For example, back in the days before social media, actors were the influencers of the day. Not only were they paid to be on stage, but they also made a considerable amount of cash by filming commercials, making surprise appearances, and promoting products at a store. In the social media age, that category of influencer has largely merged with the ones you'll find on social media and utilize it to further their influence. Everyone from newscasters, reality TV stars, announcers, musicians, and athletes has a major social media account and uses it regularly to promote and spread their influence.

The job of an influencer is to catch the attention of the people following his or her page. Simply put, attention means promotion. Paid collaborations with brands, companies, and their brands and companies are the daily grind for the influencer. The hope is that by creating traffic, sales will increase. As an influencer, using the term not strictly in a social media sense, your job is to take the assets available to you online and offline and get your name out there. The goal is to create a sense of reciprocity with the follower.

Many people hold the title of an influencer at some point in their careers. For example, athletes could advertise and promote products between games and training to make additional cash as influencers. An influencer could also be a social media star, actor, musician, or TV/online show's host.

How Influencers Make Money

The revenue made from being an influencer is mostly from percentages from sales he or she generates. With the products they endorse, like any business, influencers need a clear-cut plan to have revenue and be profitable. This is not an easy task and requires following trends on many different accounts, buying and featuring products, and often launching their brands.

Monetization is available on most social media platforms and has clear-cut methods easily learned. However, there's often a lack of specialty with being an influencer. You may have a niche like travel or fashion, but it's not usually a learned skill that you then turn around and sell as a service. Maybe it's posing wearing the latest Nikes or new up-and-coming business workout shorts. This portion of an influencer's monetization comes from how many followers he or she can expose to the product—the greater the influence, the higher the price for endorsing.

The influencer also utilizes affiliate marketing and other advertisement-centric methods. This involves using links to connect his or her followers with a featured product . Each time that link is used to purchase one of the items, the influencer receives a small fee for that follower using the link. Many influencers use promotions to boost this process, but the formula is pretty standard: use your influence to direct the followers to a product or service. As long as he or she can generate consistent traffic, the influencer should make money.

The client base is large for an influencer. Suppose you think about what kinds of products are typically featured in influencer media and on what platforms influencers often appear (ads online, social media, TV ads). In that case, it's understandable that the pool of individuals they market to is fairly wide. The influencer has to cast a wide net, as the statistics on how many people purchase products promoted by influencers can be pretty bleak. The average influencer needs to attract eight to nine people for every closed deal, which simply means purchased product. While algorithms may usually show ads to specific accounts, narrowing the process down to a specific population is difficult. The influencer must maintain heavy traffic over his or her content to make his or her business model profitable.

The influencer does not own the product or service, in most cases, and promotes his or her influence. This makes it difficult for the influencer to control what happens with a product or service unless he or she launches his or her brand or business. If you've seen a celebrity go from selling other brands' perfumes to one day starting his or her line of fragrances, this is what has happened. He or she has transitioned from being strictly influential in these cases.

The role of an influencer is a coveted position these days. It looks to many people to be a life that involves travel, maybe some modeling, lots of free products, and short work hours, where your lifestyle is what makes you money. The problem is that this simply isn't the case for most influencers. The average influencer has trouble generating traffic and spends more than full-time hours generating income. While many become successful and live a fulfilling life, many more become disillusioned by the exhausting lifestyle and give up along the way. It can be a demanding role that does not allow for a good work-life balance. The inability to disconnect can make many tired of generating income this way.

Experts

What Is an Expert?

The expert is someone who has mastered a certain craft or trade. Generally, I think of professors when I think of an expert. They know a lot about a specific field and enjoy teaching others. Still, they are confined to the web developers, marketers, and business developers—all fall under the label of being an expert. The expert uses the tools he or she has mastered to cater to a clientele specifically looking for the subject that is his or her specialty. He or she then monetizes his or her skills and performs services or produces goods to receive payment.

Expert have to rely on clients needing or wanting their specific skills. Depending on their marketing capabilities, the expert may or may not gather a good group of clients to make the revenue they need. They will need to go out and engage with potential clients to have work. This may look like a gig-work site like Fiverr, job board, website, or ads. The marketing process will look different depending on the specialty. If a particular expert's services cannot be remotely performed or long distance, he or she will have to rely on his or her local community to supply the demand for his or her product.

Experts have framed their business to service a specific core set of clients. This is where they have monetized their skills and where most of their business originates. However, the group of clients the expert works with is niche and unique. It varies depending on the expert's specialty but consistently is a narrow population of clients. This can make the role of an expert both simple and complicated at the same time. It's simple to provide the service needed, but it isn't easy to specialize in a broad-enough niche to apply to a large clientele that can sustain a consistent workflow.

What Do Experts Do?

The role of experts is simple. They complete a certain task they are specially trained for. Suppose we expand the definition to contain all forms of experts. In that case, that would include athletes who play a professional sport, programmers who design websites, musicians who play for a symphony, music producers, business specialists, accountants, doctors, lawyers—anyone specially trained for a topic or certain subject.

More fundamentally, the experts complete a task with special knowledge. For example, if you quit your nine to five to open a handmade furniture business and construct tables and chairs in your shop, you are an expert. Your expertise lies in something you can uniquely do well. This differentiates you from the competition because to succeed, you have to be doing that unique task better than the competition. You specialize over time, get good at making that furniture, and you're likely to charge more and may see sales go higher and higher. The ultimate goal is to corner a certain market and maintain a consistent clientele through that skill set.

The expert caters to an audience that is narrow and well defined. The clientele he or she services most likely needs his or her specific set of skills. There is probably not much the expert does outside of that skill set. Experts are also somewhat inhibited from pivoting because their focus is defined and set by the specialty. After years of education and work in one specific niche, any transition can be difficult and disrupting to the expert's life.

Another option the expert has is to teach his or her specialty. Outside of utilizing his or her skills to generate income, the expert can teach others the same skill set. This could look like an online course, one-on-one training, or even writing a book about the process. When we observe what makes an authority a more profitable possibility than an expert, we'll discuss how this ability to teach this skill comes in handy as the expert transitions to authority.

Teaching is a great way for the expert to break out of his or her daily work, making it a popular option for someone who has been in the industry for many years. A prime example of this is seen in many business schools. Frequently, after an accountant, financial advisor, or marketing manager has been in the industry for many years, he or she will begin teaching courses at universities on the side. This is another method of how an expert can monetize his or her specialty.

How Do Experts Make Money?

The expert is a role that mostly monetizes on knowledge. Most likely, he or she has valuable knowledge in one specific niche, where he or she gets his or her income. He or she could have gained that knowledge in college, trade school, boot camps, seminars, or is simply self-taught. Whatever the subject of expertise, his or her marketability centers on outperforming competitors. He or she differentiates him or herself with skills and market, with that differentiation being his or her skill set.

The good news for the expert is that if he or she can do a good enough job in that niche, he or she can bring in pretty decent revenue. The problem is that the process begins and ends with the expert. He or she is the one bringing the skills to the table. This puts more pressure on him or her than on influencers because the product starts and ends with him or her. If the expert fail at developing his or her product, then he or she is liable. The influencer just needs to make sure he or she markets well enough and maintain his or her influential status. He or she doesn't have to design and specialize in making money, which is one of the biggest differences.

As experts develop their skills, they can expect to make more money over time. They grow their skills and maybe even acquire more skills within their niche with the hopes of raising their marketability. The tasks they complete are the key to monetization. As long as they can complete their service, then they will most likely make money. This makes the role a simple path to high returns that correlates with how much time the expert puts into his or her work.

While they can generate high returns, experts are by no means exempt from struggles related to generating income. The life of an expert can either have high client engagement with high-income capabilities, or it can have low engagement with much lower profits to show. In addition, due to saturated markets, experts can find themselves in a competitive role requiring a competition of capability and skill to gain more orders and leads than a competing expert.

Which Are You?

Now that you understand what makes an expert and an influencer, which category best currently describes you? In the future, it will be important to know what areas of your skill set you need to strengthen. In addition, knowing which role you are currently playing can help you understand why you may be struggling to reach your full potential and how you can work to improve those areas.

Many of you have probably heard of Gary Vaynerchuk. He is worth quite a lot of money and has established himself as one of this generation's biggest voices in entrepreneurship. While he enjoys that status now as an authority in business, marketing, and new trends, he was not always the authority he is today. His parents, who immigrated from Belarus, owned a family wine business that sold their wine out of a regular brick-and-mortar storefront. Vaynerchuk saw that this model wasn't taking advantage of the many online growing markets and decided to open an online wine store.

While his story seems simple, it isn't. The "small" shift he took when he decided to take his parent's business online was life-changing. At the time, no one understood why you needed to sell wine online. He launched an online channel called Wine Library TV on YouTube and created an entirely new front for the marketing capabilities of his family's company. Wine Library began selling and shipping wine online and daily featured their different wines.

The story of Wine Library shows a strong understanding of where his company stood. Vaynerchuk knew that they were positioned well as a wine store, making them more or fewer wine experts, but it was that additional step he took to differentiate them from any other brand that drove the company to millions more in revenue and propelled him into a life that has helped many young entrepreneurs' careers. By gaining exposure from starting

Wine Library and sharing his knowledge with people worldwide, Vaynerchuk was able to set himself apart as an expert. He was able to take with him even after he left his parents to start on his own. Now he is an accomplished author, speaker, and is featured almost daily worldwide on podcasts, YouTube channels, and radio. This entire journey started with a strong understanding of his company's position and how to leverage influence to drive his company and life into a position of lasting authority.

Vaynerchuk's story is one of the most powerful examples of understanding your path to authority. It's crucial to know now what the path to gaining authority will look like and expand your knowledge in that area that you feel your business or personal career lacks. Knowing what category best describes you can also help you better understand the progress you need to see and help you create milestones on your way to success.

A good question to ask yourself would be: With your current standing and following, what are you good at, and do people in your circle view you as the go-to person on that subject?

In today's world, meaningful differences between businesses are rarely rooted in price or product, but instead in customer experience.

—JAY BAER

5

The Elements of Influence

Influence is a critical component of your authority. To build your network, get your name out there among your peers, and boost your marketability, you need influence. Your influence is a strong characteristic that becomes a necessary asset when pursuing authority. It's how everyone already knows who you are when you walk into a room. I've been around some amazing speakers, athletes, and artists, and I can tell you that it's strange the kind of presence these people carry when they walk into a room. The atmosphere changes, all of a sudden, wherever they're standing in the center of the room. This is the kind of presence that gets you in front of newspapers and magazines.

In the process of achieving authority, there is a strong need to expand your influence. If you're already someone who enjoys a very strong influential presence, I'd still encourage you to read this portion as there are likely elements of influence that you have not considered before. The expert will want to park on this chapter for a while to understand how to take his or her expertise and skills and use them to create a

Influence consists of four major elements:

- Reciprocity;
- Consistency;
- Social proof; and
- Personal brand.

The authority takes from the elements those that will propel the services he or she specializes into the next level of recognition. For an authority to understand how to gain notoriety and how to market him or herself,

The value of being an influencer is the ability to create a customer experience. The elements of an influencer all work together to make the influencer able to create a customer experience that leaves a lasting impression on that customer. The business of an influencer is to make heads turn and grab the attention of the consumer. When you consider how hard it is to draw in a potential client and close a deal, it makes sense that the influencer has to possess the ability to make a lasting impression. These elements we'll cover are what make an influencer unique.

Reciprocity

Have you ever felt so good about how an ad or spokesperson made you feel that you almost felt obligated to purchase the product? Just because of how you were made to feel, you were willing to spend money. This is called reciprocity, and it's an amazing part of how influence works. It's the desire to reciprocate the positive feeling that an ad or influencer gives you by purchasing the goods or service.

Maybe it was the humor or song in the ad. Maybe it was the funny tagline or simply the extremely good deal they were offering you. Whatever the reason, you felt the need to return that good deed back, and it convinced you to part ways with several dollars to do so. This process is what drives many ad campaigns and marketing strategies and is considered a highly effective method.

Reciprocity is an incredibly powerful tool. It can create such a strong feeling that it can create brand loyalty for life. The feeling that many people get when they develop a brand familiarity is strong enough to cause many people to swear off similar products of a different brand. If you secure reciprocity with your clients, you can

It's a strong asset if you know how to utilize reciprocity to your advantage. The refreshing thing about this reciprocity is that you can generate revenue and push sales simply by doing good things for people and by creating value. You don't have to deal in anything shady or any pushy marketing. The pushing is all done by the comfort people get by making a purchase in your store or on your website. This is the process of using social good to drive your sales. For a professional or maybe for a consultant, reciprocity presents in the form of your being trusted with the business of the company or individual hiring you for your services. You are then creating even more reciprocity by adding one more name in your portfolio of satisfied customers.

Reciprocity can be invoked by offering a sale on services or offering an exchange of products/services. It can also be invoked by an honest explanation about how the company works through transparency. There are few limits on the possibilities when it comes to reciprocity. This element of influence is absolutely necessary to expand your influence.

Why Is Reciprocity Necessary?

The necessity of reciprocity is largely due to the powerful effect it has on a customer. Creating a good image and keeping that good image is no small task but can reap huge benefits in terms of sales due to reciprocity. Anyone learning the elements of influence needs to approach it as an asset that they need to acquire before they hope to expand their influence.

While there are many powerful features of influence that can propel business and products into recognition, reciprocity is that feature that is intensely strong in its ability to retain customer loyalty from seemingly nothing. Loyalty generated from reciprocity is a strong kind of loyalty that you can't buy or push on people by optimizing your ads on Instagram or spamming their inbox with emails. It requires tact and a strong understanding of yourself, your product, and the clients you are serving.

Consistency

At twenty years old, I knew that the one human need that I wanted to help people with was to give them a voice. I wanted to help people feel popular; I wanted to help them grow their influence. So I asked myself, *How can I help people?* That's when I started Kivo Daily. After doing it for Paul for several years, I knew it was time to do it for others. The unique thing about digital marketing is the consistency it requires. Yes, it is easy to pay for an ad or article and get people to see your brand, but it doesn't stop there. The statistic is that a consumer has to see your brand or commercial eight to nine times before he or she pulls the trigger. This is an easy topic to understand. You don't go to the gym once; you have to go several times. You don't wash your hair once; you do it several times a week.

In the world of influence, consistency is king. There is nothing that boosts your posts and updates like a consistent stream of content. I remember when people began vlogging on YouTube on a daily basis. The commitment that must have taken for many of them is completely insane, but it has paid off for many of them. A new post, posted at the same time every day for a year, is an insane amount of content. The same can be said for the consistency of emails, tweets, and ads. The importance of consistency is not limited to a digital space. In your own actions, people are more likely to trust the brand of someone who is consistent than of someone who is constantly changing his or her approach and essentially rebranding on a regular basis. Your actions and words need to remain consistent for your brand to grow its follower and client base.

Social Proof

Social proof is what boosts brands. It's the practice of seeing someone who is an expert at something promoting an item related to his or her specialty. The act of imitating the behavior we see in an advertisement is acting on social proof. If you prefer to wear a certain kind of activewear because a celebrity was wearing it in an advertisement, then you are acting on the social proof. While I was writing this book, I had the opportunity to do several news interviews. It was an awesome experience for me, but more importantly, it was a huge boost to my brand. Think about it. Who are you going to hire if they message you? Someone you have never seen or the guy you saw talking about business on TV? That's the power of social proof.

Think about it some more. Most of us prefer a certain brand when it comes to our phones: Apple or Samsung. There are others, but these are the top-selling phones in the world. Now, both phones are well made. Both can call, text, and take photos, but we all decide to choose a certain phone. How did we come to that choice? Most of us don't go around testing each kind of smartphone before we buy it, so we ask around. We ask our friends if they got the newest version and how it performed for them, we look at their response to features on the phone, and we Google the expert's opinions online.

An example of social proof is found in celebrity endorsements. This looks like an MMA fighter advertising for a stick deodorant or a runner appearing in an advertisement for an energy drink. What their presence brings to the table is the social proof that this item is, in fact, great for this use, and it's so good that I actually use it. It doesn't have to be a direct celebrity endorsement, though. It could simply be a friend or neighbor using a product and having a positive opinion of it.

This is one of the most valuable tools in the influencer's bag. The ability to appear in a picture or video and cause the sales of that item to go up is an incredible concept, and it's one that makes influencers a lot of money. A well-known form of social proof is to create it by using celebrities that people trust to create a sense of familiarity with the product.

While social proof is amazing, there is a negative side to it as well. Social proof can be a problem for a business too. As much as it can mean positive peer pressure to go and do something, it can also be negative peer pressure to avoid something. The wisdom of the crowd can quickly sway, and when it does, it can be the end of many products and brands. There have been millions of dollars lost in sales due to instances of boycotts, unethical manufacturing problems, and, in many cases, simply from trends going in a different direction. As quickly as the consumers can go along with a product because "everyone is getting one," they can just as quickly lose interest because "no one buys those anymore." You need to avoid social proof like this at all costs!

The trick with social proof is to create a positive sense of proof around your products and services. Show that what you offer is something anyone would be happy to try. You're not demonizing those who don't purchase your product in these cases. You're simply creating social proof for people and giving people the confidence they are making a worthwhile purchase. The advantage influencers have is that they are accustomed to following social trends and participating in creating commentary or buzz around a topic. With practice in this area, it's just a matter of using that experience to capitalize on those trends and using them to create social proof around your product or service.

As an influencer, you are constantly trying to provide social proof. By providing social proof, you're ensuring your income. You're giving a sense of legitimacy to something that is not necessarily better than a competing product. To do that, you need people to see how truly unique it is. In a sense, you are not necessarily creating demand, more like pipelining it from the general demand for that kind of product to demand your specific product or the product you represent.

Personal Brand

If you're in any position of influence, you'll find that a personalized brand can do a lot to differentiate you from the competition. I'm not talking about launching a line of cigars with your name on them or a perfume fragrance named after you. I'm referring to branding your services and influence in the form of a name or logo. As a personal example, my name is Dillon Kivo, but many of my clients recognize my services as falling under the Authority Titans brand. A personal brand can do many things for you. It can:

- Create brand recognition;
- Boost your monetization capabilities;
- Create a sense of scarcity; and
- Create a sense of contrast.

I want to mainly focus on the last two: scarcity and contrast. What exactly do those mean in the context of personal branding, and why are they important to the influencer?

Scarcity

A personal brand creates a sense of scarcity for the services you offer. It takes your services and places them under your name. If you look around for other companies that offer similar services, there are probably thousands, but the sense of scarcity comes in that there is only one with your name attached to it. The level of quality you provide will come to be associated with that brand, for better or worse, and the brand then becomes the only brand that carries that exact quality of service.

I don't think scarcity is too difficult a concept, but it's one that we all don't think about enough. Imagine a fast-food chain (we won't name any in particular). Once you picture that chain, you probably have a certain location in mind. You can imagine the logo, service you received there, whether it was dirty or clean, your food was cold or hot, and the list goes on, but it's those experiences that you attach to that chain. Was it positive? If so, you probably feel positively toward that brand. Was it negative? Unless you've had other experiences that were positive enough to negate one bad experience, you probably carry a negative image associated with that brand. Scarcity

This is why your character and influence are so incredibly important in the influential portion of this process. The experience you provide for your clients will be linked to your brand name, your name, or your company's name. It's easy to mess up a client experience but very difficult to mend. So make sure that the concept of scarcity doesn't cause him or her to go and view another brand as the only one for him or her.

If you're considering specializing, which I highly recommend, it will serve you well to establish a brand that represents the service your clients can expect from you. Remember what is at stake but also to gain. Immediate recognition is a powerful tool for influence, and when used properly, can save money and time in the long term. With such quick recognition, the need to heavily market goes away, and you're able to focus more on the customer and services being provided. A great example of this would be someone who has already become a celebrity and now is venturing into advertising products on social media and TV ads. He has plenty of experience and is very good at what he does. When offering to market a product, he will likely gain immediate attention and generate sales due to social proof. There's only one of him; he knows that anyone else doesn't match with his theme, so theft asks the celebrity to come back to shoot a photoshoot for them. This celebrity had a shortcut in the form of a position on the floor. I can't speak on the content of his work. The sense of scarcity of not getting the one and only celebrity with his name and features makes them reconsider doing it again.

In this context, scarcity also includes promotional material. Creating scarcity in some inventory is another way to roll out more of that product and get it sold at a high yield price as the supply is technically short. This is the idea behind fire sales. While it doesn't always have to be that urgent of a sale, the idea of a sales week or a sales month would be great too!

Creating a sense of scarcity through a brand name is an influential move that serves to create a sense of urgency to acquire your product or use your services. Scarcity helps you benefit from the buyer who doesn't think there are any other brands like yours around. It's this scarcity that causes buyers to ensure that if they're going to buy a certain good or service, they're going to do it with your brand, not any others. If your brand is identical to the surrounding brands in the market, then you don't have much to offer your clients. This is why scarcity is exactly what a strong brand needs to stay pertinent to their clients and necessary to their clients who have established brand loyalty.

Contrast

Another major product of a strong personal brand is a sense of contrast. In this context, contrast refers to the difference between two items that are slightly different being perceived as drastically different. Another way of referring to this concept is "perceptual contrast," referring to the fact that there's a difference in how we perceive two items. The contrast between the two different brands is most likely due to the labeling, logos, and story behind the brand; so little of it is the actual products. The style and look of the product you produce are all included and are a direct reflection of the rest of your branding.

This is an incredibly powerful concept that helps us understand why two pairs of shoes that are essentially built the same are perceived to be so different by the consumer. If you're a fan of sneakers and compare a pair of Adidas with a pair of Nike sneakers, you'll more than likely think there's a significant difference between the two, and I can promise you it's not because one is built that much better than the other. The reason is most accurately attributed to the difference in how we perceive the two, and it's all because of the logo.

The brand dictates the difference. Building a personal brand can make you into a competitive influence and differentiate you from others, even though your services could be almost identical. You'll work hard at differentiating through performance, and you may legitimately perform twice as well as the competition. You may be able to close leads at a rate that is two to three times your competitors, but with a brand, you are able to make that difference much more than by image alone. The brand you start becomes a direct reflection of your values and can include whatever products or services you are currently working on.

Don't start a company unless it's an obsession and something you love. If you have an exit strategy, it is not an obsession.

—MARK CUBAN

CHAPTER 6

The Elements of Expertise

The modern world has no shortage of experts. If you go online to sites that provide gig work, like Fiverr or Upwork, you're going to see them everywhere. There are digital marketing experts, web development, educators—the list goes on. I guarantee you that if you or your business have some specific need, there's someone out there who can fill it. I would say that most of these people have a strong degree of expertise in their field.

Historically, the title expert comes with the experience of working in one's field and the ability to capitalize on that advanced knowledge. There'd be no bridges, medications or treatments, or huge societal gaps that would exist without experts. So we're going to define what makes an expert in this chapter and how a true understanding of expertise can help you in the process of establishing authority.

Who Is an Expert?

When I say expert, I'm sure many titles come to mind, depending on who you are. Maybe it's a doctor, lawyer, or professor. On the other hand, if you're into sports, it could be the names of analysts who discuss team stats or an athlete who has trained his or her whole life for one position or role. So we're going to define what I mean when I say an expert and get a better understanding of how you or the experts you may know fit into this category.

Who falls under the category of expert? To fully utilize your expertise when pursuing authority, you must clearly define expertise. I could give you the dictionary definition of it, but I'd rather just tell you how I am using the term. Going forward, when we discuss the experts, we're talking about people who are simply in a role where they have more advanced knowledge about a subject. The expert has specific skills that we'll discuss in depth later. They're the ones with the training and education required to carry out specialized actions to make money. This could be real estate agents, programmers, marketers, writers, videographers, or athletes. There are so many people that fall under this category that an exhaustive list would be too long, and I'm not just talking about college graduates that studied a topic either. Experts, by whatever process, have come to a point where they could give advice on a certain subject and, for our purposes, could monetize this skill.

You're probably wondering how this concept applies to you. Well, in the process of achieving authority, it's important to be known as an expert. If you are not an expert, this means you need to grow your skill set or improve the skills you already have. If you want authority, you can't skip steps and simply fake that you have skills. Integrity aside, today's job market has reviews, quick communication, and almost-instant feedback on your performance. To be known as an authority in your field, you have to first be one. There are no shortcuts to the authority status, and that is true for any field and niche. The ultimate proof is results, and the results are difficult to come by, but that's true for anything worth having. So don't worry; we'll see in the coming chapters how easily attainable each individual step is and how the total process is merely the sum of its steps.

As an example from my own life, I have launched several companies in the PR world. These days, I am considered an expert in that field and have been interviewed as a business analyst on PR and marketing subjects. At the beginning of my career, this area of expertise needed a lot of fine-tuning. I would have never made it this far if I didn't take my lifelong education and personal development seriously. It doesn't have to come from a university or a paid-for course. While those certifications can help prove your expertise, the most important part is mental growth and refusing to only have a shallow understanding of your skills and business. Knowing more and going deeper creates interest, and interest is what drives understanding.

An Expert with Authority

In this chapter, I want to walk you through a crucial step in establishing your authority: establishing your expertise. To get you to that point, we're going to cover six main points that should help simplify the process of achieving the status of an expert for you. The main points you need to develop in establishing your expertise are:

- Mastery;
- Consistency;
- Social proof;
- Skill;
- Knowledge; and
- Experience.

In developing these areas, you'll become fully rounded as an expert and be able to present your expertise as an authority. We're going to cover each element and take a look at how they all tie together. The elements of authority are the steps you will need to understand in depth before you can understand how to exercise your authority.

The first element of expertise we will cover is mastery. Mastery is the most basic fundamental element of expertise and is only accomplished through dedication to a craft or business. The mark of a true expert is a mastery of his or her niche that defines how he or she operates his or her business. To be considered an expert, you have to gain mastery, and that is a highly misunderstood concept. The general thoughts about mastery are that it comes with years of experience and education, but you'd be surprised how many people spend years of their lives practicing the same subject only to be upstaged by someone much less experienced who happened to know something that the expert who had been working in that niche for years had never considered.

What matters with mastery is the ability to perform the skill better than the average person. This doesn't have to come with years of experience but does require a deep understanding. There's a reason businesses pay consultants tons of money to assess their marketing and operations. The money saved or made in the long run is much more than the price they pay to have their businesses improved by an expert who has mastered his or her niche.

There is a misconception you'll see coming up over and over again if you spend any time in a niche market, and that's the idea that you must have a set amount of experience to be considered a master at something. There's this idea that mastery only comes with time and that unless you've spent years on a certain subject, you aren't able to master it like someone who has spent those years. This may be true for some things, but in my life, I have seen incredibly young people who have put in the hours necessary to understand and master a specialty, and they did not need years in that industry.

For true mastery, what is most important is approaching your work with the mindset of quality. If you aspire for quality in your work and make that your goal, not making money on or creating a business out of it, then you will be able to master the elements of your niche that many have told you will take years to develop. The mark of the master is his or her results, not his or her perceived excellence. It doesn't matter if you give off the impression that you are a master at your skill; unless you turn that skill into the best version of itself, you're still a novice. It doesn't take as long as they say for you to take your interests and master them. It only takes dedication.

Consistency

Consistency is a necessary element of expertise. The expert needs consistency to make his or her product a marketable feature of his or her business. Without consistency, the expert will find that his or her clientele and their peers will not only lose respect for his or her work but will doubt his or her expertise as well. It's with consistency that the expert differentiates his or her product from the competition and provides him or herself with a reputation that will last through different client experiences. The average client simply wants the same product that he or she saw produced for a previous client and looks to the expert to deliver that same experience for him or her.

The expert provides a consistent product, or he or she is not taken seriously as an expert. Consistency is a mark of a true expert. Rather than getting lucky and creating the perfect product once, the expert knows how to consistently provide the necessary skill to create the perfect product over and over again, like an assembly line. This isn't something you do with random sprints of energy. It's a pattern you develop over time. To create your own luck, you have to create a schedule of productivity that will allow you to produce whatever service or product you specialize in on a regular basis. This makes your expertise a consistent process.

Making your product showcase your best work on a consistent basis is the mark of a true expert. When growing your expertise, you have to practice perfectly to make your work perfect. This is true for customer satisfaction as well as for marketing purposes. As an expert, personal testimonies are what will drive sales for you. If those reviews are not matching up with your product or if you are making consistent mistakes that are hurting your reviews, then your revenue and growth are going to suffer.

Social Proof

Social proof is another crucial element of expertise. The expert needs to create a sense of social proof to become marketable for his or her expertise. While there are many products and services that are easily rated good or poorly done, the market is also full of products that require a general consensus as to the quality of a product. This could be a product that is not different from competing brands. The differentiating factor is the general opinion of the product. Social proof is where reviews come into play heavily. The opinions of old customers and clients will either drive sales in the future or stagnate the returns the business experiences.

For example, let's use a trendy restaurant that just opened up on the corner—there are way too many trendy restaurants in my neighborhood. I don't understand the attraction. The food was mediocre at best, and the atmosphere was uncomfortable at times. However, if you ask anyone in that area, they would tell you it's one of the hottest new places to eat, and then it's absolutely a great place to go while you're in town. You may not necessarily be interested in the food, but there is a generally positive opinion of this restaurant, so you go. This is an example of social proof in action, and it is exactly why testimonials are so important to the expert. If you're an expert and pursuing social proof, get testimonials. They'll do more good for you than any expensive marketing campaign ever could. Testimonials are one of the most effective ways to generate optimal social proof for your business.

Social proof creates demand, and experts create social proof. The use of social proof is essential if the expert wants to create a sense of demand for his or her product. If there is enough buzz, if there is a general consensus, and it's a positive consensus, then the product will most likely be accepted by most consumers. The problem most experts face is creating social proof, to begin with. There are many methods to do this, and most are about as good as the other. Find out what works best for your product, but whatever you do, come away with a strong sense of social proof for your product. It will do a lot to create momentum, but you have to give it a chance to do so by generating it, to begin with.

To make social proof work for you as the expert, engagement is everything. Directly engaging the clients can help show that client loyalty is rewarded and appreciated, and complaints or concerns will be taken seriously. What this looks like is a response to a direct review on any of the major platforms. Direct response on a Google review can show those considering your business or service that you care about your brand enough to engage and fix the issues your customers have faced. Many people have been turned away by a few negative reviews that went unanswered. I would go as far as to say having no issues with a business creates even less loyalty than having an issue that is addressed and validated. I think most people understand that mistakes will happen, and performance issues may arise at some point, but a validating response to a client can give the expert a solid testimonial that can develop a strong sense of social proof.

Skill

Skill is another key element of expertise. It characterizes how the expert is different from the influencer. They are experienced and knowledgeable about skills, and that skill is what ultimately makes money for them. The skills you possess may be something you are an expert at, or they may simply be something you happen to know how to do but are not very skilled at. In the end, both the influencer and expert are skilled, technically. The expert possesses abilities that are more traditionally considered skills, and the influencer has influential capabilities to market. Either way, the methods they use to gain a profit are considered skills that the experts use to make their living. There is a lot that can be done to expand a skill set as an expert and a lot that can be done to learn particular skills even deeper, but the skills that matter the most are the ones that differentiate the expert from their competition.

To become an expert or grow your expertise, you must have the necessary skills. If you don't have them, you need to make sure you are in the process of growing your skill set and learning what you need to learn. The ability to adapt and develop their skills is what will keep experts going and what will keep them profitable. Without any skills, they aren't much of an expert.

It's important to find the skill interesting to you. If you're in the process of developing your expertise and find that the skills you are learning, while interesting, are not exactly what you want to be good at, just necessary for growth and expanding your influence, then there are many ways to hack your process to make yourself more likely to drive forward within that skill set. The way this works is that you consider the skill you are striving to understand better, and you show yourself how it fits into your business structure.

If you are working to understand how you can become an expert, the best way to know is to try and develop your skills. If you're finding this hard to do, there are many online educational tools and mentors that could teach you how you can take simple things like writing, photography, music production, and so on and make the most amazing small businesses out of them.

All you need to do is be willing to identify the skill you want to expand and push to understand it better.

Knowledge

Another important element of expertise is knowledge. Knowledge is what you apply to your specialty to make yourself a true expert. This is how you develop your expertise. When experts market their business or services, a point of value for them to showcase is their knowledge in the subject they are considered an expert in.

Knowledge is how experts obtains their position, to begin with. To have been established as experts, to begin with, they must have proven a deep knowledge and understanding of a niche subject. This knowledge is the proof of expertise if it's coupled with quality work. It can be taught, explained, and used as a monetized product.

Knowledge is what people pay for. Online courses are everywhere and almost every subject you could think of, and definitely, a few you and I have never thought of. In an increasingly specialized market, you're going to continue to see this to be the case. People will pay for education and will definitely pay for someone who is educated in a specialty. The number of things a business owner needs to keep track of is too many for him or her to specialize in each subject. Many will pay for education, but when it comes to getting a task done, they pay for the educated.

Experience

The final element of expertise is experience. This element isn't surprising to see as experience is something we usually look for in someone who is working as an expert. The element of experience shows the consumer that the expert is not only skillful but also has the know-how that comes with having worked in his or her niche for a period of time

Experience proves an expert's legitimacy. The legitimate expert has not only studied the subject but has carried out the actions required to solidify that knowledge. They say that only about 10 percent of what you know about a subject comes from learning it the first time. The remaining 90 percent comes from repetition, on-the-job practice, and carrying out the actions required to commit the details that you've learned to memory. There's no mistake that even with all of the education on earth, an expert can still be considered a novice unless he or she has had the opportunity to put his or her learning to practice to prove his or her legitimacy.

Experience solidifies the expert's ability and position. When looking for new clients and trying to expand their business, experts may find that they have trouble doing so without enough experience. An expert without experience isn't going to be seen as a reputable source of expertise when compared to one with experience. On the other hand, the expert who has plenty of experience can easily establish his or her expertise with the proof coming from his or her experience. This can save you time and energy in the long run by giving you the ability to market using your experience. This isn't to say that the expert who has been in his or her role for a long period of time is automatically more skilled. True expertise doesn't come with just time, and the time experts spend in their niche needs to be well spent and for their skills to be fully developed. With good experience, experts can master their niche. They can become who everyone goes to when they need advice and can become who everyone sends their business to. This experience is necessary to continue to expand their clientele, which, in turn, will not only expand their business but will ensure that their business continues to thrive.

The need for experience can be a problem for the influencer. The influencer needs to gain that experience by training, working in that niche, or by putting him or herself in a position to learn about that niche from someone else with experience. Without it, transitioning out of a solely influential role and into one that requires experience will prove difficult for the influencer. If you're considering moving into that kind of role, the good news for you is that there are many opportunities in today's economy to take classes, courses, or boot camps to try and understand the market in which you are working to develop expertise.

If somebody offers you an amazing opportunity, but you are not sure you can do it—say yes, then learn how to do it later.

—RICHARD BRANSON

CHAPTER 7

The Downfall

The Downfall

The world is full of experts and influencers. Both of those categories are filled with people who are successful and have made a fulfilling life for themselves. I'd be lying if I told you you'd absolutely fail in either category, but these aren't easy roles to fill and often require much more time than they are worth. There's a better way to succeed.

While you may find success as an expert or influencer, the downfall of these roles is that you're unlikely to succeed, and if you do, it will not be overnight. The careers of athletes, musicians, and other experts take years to cultivate and train. Influencers have to spend so much of their time chasing recognition and fame, only to lose it if they fall off a trend or don't pay to boost their ads and endorsements. We could agree that's hardly a secure plan.

Back before I started working for Paul, I was training to be a hockey player. Like any other guy who is working toward that kind of goal, I was determined to succeed in my sport, and my training reflected that. Not to brag, but I wasn't a bad player. Other guys had done it and went from nothing to the front of sports magazines. I knew that if I trained hard enough, I could and would make it there too, but that didn't work out the way I planned it. There came the point when I realized that my chances of actually making it to the NHL were fairly low. I was just a tiny bit too slow and slightly not talented enough. So I made, what at the time was, a very difficult decision. I quit hockey.

When I left behind the dream of being in the NHL, I realized it was time to find my next thing. I still had a burning desire to be the best at whatever I decided to do, but I wasn't sure what that was. Looking back, that wasn't a bad place to be. I've seen countless guys continue chasing a dream of professional sports only to find themselves past their prime and leaving a pretty obscure life. That's because we are so in love with the grind of working hard and chasing the dream. I remember working my tail off training as a hockey player for that same opportunity. I trained hard and had all the confidence in the world that I was going to make it to the pros and would have a long career ahead of me. There'd be endorsements, interviews, travel, all of the things you associate with a career in a professional sport, but none of that happened for me, and it doesn't happen for most players.

What's interesting to me is to watch players that do make it. I mean, you look at guys like Lebron James or Steph Curry in the NBA. They are arguably the best at their sports, but they don't stay there. They take their expertise and branch out to other sports, business ventures, anything that keeps building upon what they have already established. The players that fail to do so quickly lose all their wealth *and* influence because they failed to establish themselves as an authority.

As only an expert or influencer, you are limiting your potential. There is so much more to your potential than simply generating revenue for an executive that owns your gig, job app, or the paid job board. I'm not saying these aren't legitimate ways to make a living. You can promote products on social media for endorsement fees. You can find creative jobs online and heavily compete for them. I'd like to stop here and take a look at why this grind can be a poor use of your abilities and potential. There's a better way, and to understand how much better it is, we first need to look at what problems we're avoiding here.

The Downfall of the Expert

The expert faces many struggles in his or her careers. The many different people in this category sacrifice hours and days of their lives to achieve success when they could be making much more in a shorter period of time. The problem I have observed is that the years they have put into learning their niche is almost never awarded per its value. There is always a part of the market that is trying to take their profits down a notch and make it harder for them to take home what they deserve.

This category is undervalued and stuck because their expertise is in the tasks they complete, not the process of selling that task to a potential client. The expert may be hesitant to over-market him or herself. Maybe they are insecure about their skills, or maybe they simply think their skills should be sufficient to get them to work. While that may be true, and while their skills should be sufficient to gain meaningful employment, they more often than not do not provide this. More often than not, the expert faces a market of harsh competition, price wars, and a constant threat of being less specialized and less skilled than a nearby competitor.

The market is saturated with programmers and marketers, business consultants, and copywriters. There is no shortage of experts, and they end up competing with each other, which makes it difficult for the individual expert to get work. This is where the downsides of the expert are pretty heavy. The job market starts becoming a matter of price, which makes perfectly good experts who are highly skilled have to lower their prices and compete. You don't want to get into a price war. The loser is almost always the expert. No matter how specialized you are, there is always someone who can undercut you and stay profitable, no matter how much he or she lowers his or her prices. This isn't the kind of environment you want to find yourself in, and it's definitely not the environment you want to try and promote a business in. Staying out of heavily saturated markets is always a good idea, but as an expert, staying out of them may not be something you can so easily choose to do.

Simply relying on your expertise is not enough. The expert cannot pivot from his or her narrow clientele. The problem is that as just an expert, you're limiting your potential by pigeonholing your chances of success. The expert is stuck in his or her niche and specific clientele.

There is also the issue of social proof for the expert. With each new client, the burden of proof is on the expert to show that he or she does actually know his or her specialty and can perform well within his or her niche. Each time he or she has to remarket his or her services, he or she doesn't see much lasting social proof. This is the source of a lot of stress for many people. The hope is that they can use their hard-earned skills to serve others, but in the end, they get their legitimacy questioned and credentials scrutinized.

The Downfall of the Influencer

The problem with being an influencer is that your role doesn't require you to gain knowledge of the products and services you're representing. While you could gain more knowledge about them, there isn't much incentive to do so. The products you represent are simply there so you can present them and go on to another product. Think about the film actors you see driving a certain kind of car and talking about why they chose that car. Do you think that if they wanted to, they could design a car and maybe sell their own version? Of course, they could do that, but not with the knowledge they currently have. What is required is specialization in a skill set and knowledge of how to develop their product.

Many people have become influencers in the past several years, but not nearly as many have made it to a point where all of the time spent promoting pays off in the form of endorsement deals and affiliate income. This is not the norm, and in fact, most do not make it to this point of success. It's a legitimately difficult role to play with potentially poor payoff. Without a skill set attached, the elements of influence can fall short of delivering the impact that the influencer is trying to make. To make the best use of the influence you have and are skilled at cultivating, you're going to find you are at your best chance when you have a specialty accompanying it. This is how you go from promoting someone else's dream to promoting your own. Specialize because it will deliver the revenue you need, and please specialize your skills and make sure they are in demand. We'll say it a lot but only because it's true that your skills need to be as specialized as you can make them.

The role of an influencer comes down to living someone else's dream. As an influencer, you're spending hours working and developing your brand and presence to end up promoting someone else's dream. There's no reason this should be the case when you are already so good at promoting and marketing. No one wants to watch the profits they generate disappear up the ladder. So, put a stop to it and don't stand for it anymore. Give your influence a chance as a monetization tool. There is no reason you can't take off and start on your own now. You'd be surprised on how much you can do as an experienced influencer when you start your own business. One of the hardest parts is getting your name out there. You've already covered that for a while and will probably not have a problem promoting even further, but no matter how difficult this is, many would argue staying in a position that is being taken advantage of is even more demoralizing and harder to live with over time. Why wait until your skills are mostly burnt out? Get yourself out of the business of generating income for others and use your skills for the one who deserves to profit from them the most, and that's you.

There is also a limit to how much you can monetize as an influencer. At a certain point, the promotions only make so much, and the number of services you can offer becomes limited. This is one reason many influencers transition to owning their own brand, starting their own product line, or founding their own company. It is a great idea for those who are tired of watching their hard-earned profits going elsewhere. Unlike many other jobs, the influencer is in a uniquely good position to make this transition.

Many influencers have begun to realize that their impact is limited as well. In the same way that it's much more fulfilling to build your own dream, it's also fulfilling to work in an impactful way. If you are able to see the positive impact your work has, it will motivate you to keep working toward your goals. The unfortunate truth of influencing is that your dream and impact ultimately belong to someone else. That is the worst thing to consider, that even after all of your hard work, assets, and the rest of your work, the ultimate guide is to go right back into it, change the course your time here is taking, and make the necessary changes to put yourself back in the driver's seat. The role you play is to communicate their dream and promote it, but you're not working on anything that directly belongs to you.

The career of an influencer does not lend itself to expertise, but I guarantee you many influencers are considered experts on their products or service. For the consumer, it's a given that the person representing that product knows about it and could give information on it if asked. Yes, there are many influencers that transition from being an influencer to starting companies with the same kind of products they have been promoting, but doing so generally requires a significant learning curve. The learning curve has a tendency to make people quite early. It can be discouraging to make such a big change. In the end, the influencer is left at a disadvantage because his or her role limits his or her impact, skills, and ability to transition into a more impactful position.

The Intersection

We've seen how neither the expert nor the influencer's approach is sufficient to achieve authority. If you're an expert, you lack the ability to navigate outside of your specialty, and if you're an influencer, then you lack the specialized skill set that's needed to go professional with the products you promote. The answer for these two categories and their way of achieving authority is to adopt the practices that intersect between the two.

In the intersection, we find there are several key features of each side that contribute to a total authority in the center. The combination found here is what takes someone from one of the categories and makes him or her an authority. The authority section takes the best from each and makes a new category. These are the features of the authority:

- Consistency;
- Social proof;
- Skill;
- Knowledge; and
- Experience.

These five characteristics work together to make up a category that is skillful but has social proof, knowledge and experience, and remains consistent throughout the process and throughout the career. This is how an authority is identified and different from being merely one of the categories. The key difference between the two categories is that it takes the best parts from the other categories and leaves out the elements that are not necessary.

Focusing on these five characteristics is the key to transforming your career into a more impactful version of itself.

Influencer to Authority

The process for the influencer to gain authority starts with knowledge. While he or she already has the social proof and reciprocity, the influencer has to prioritize a deeper knowledge of his or her niche. It's this knowledge that will make a difference for him or her. If the influencer hopes to gain a strong client base and be successful as an authority, then he or she should use the influence he or she has and couple it with the newfound knowledge he or she will use to begin serving clients. Before the influencer can begin, it would be a good idea to stop and ask him or herself a few questions:

1. What skills should I be improving on in this new endeavor? To answer this, I'd recommend an in-depth analysis of the market you're entering to determine how much you'll need to expand your knowledge.

2. What pace am I going to set for myself? Learning curves can be frustrating and sometimes demoralizing. It's crucial that you set up a schedule for yourself so that you don't

burn yourself out early on and so you stay accountable and tick off those skills along the way.

3. How can these new skills be augmented by my experience as an influencer? If you already have a strong understanding of the influential side of the equation, don't let it go to waste. Use it to take the skills you have to expand and market them even further.

Using the answers to these questions, you can determine what actions you will begin taking to build your authority. If there are skill sets you need to build up, itemize them and begin working on them. The skills you would want to consider are mostly related to a specialization that becomes your point of expertise. As an influencer, your strongest point is that you can take the business you're building and further promote it. However, if you have been working in a capacity as an influencer, then you most likely are not specialized in a trade or craft. This is going to make it difficult for you to know how you will go about starting to monetize on your skills and what you will even have to offer as a product or service.

Get a good understanding of the skills you need. There is almost no end to the amount of education that is out there. Take some courses, get mentorship, and consume as much information as you can. This process will look different for everyone, but the end goal will be to take your skills and expand them to where you are considered highly specialized.

Don't worry about overspecializing either. As long as your business model remains flexible and does not require that overspecialization as its sole source of income, then you should be in a position to utilize that specialty and not have any issues with making it into an effective business model. Overspecialization is a much easier problem to solve than under specialization. Avoid being less than skilled and less than specialized, and dive straight into specializing your skills.

While developing your skills, it's important to understand the timeline you're looking at. If you are making your learning curve timeline too tight, then you are likely not going to have much success in deeply learning your topics, but if you give yourself too lenient an answer, then you run the risk of wasting valuable time. Some people procrastinate for years until they launch their first company. I am sure you don't want to be either way. So treat your timeline as a valuable asset and make yourself accountable to it. Keep your timeline as best as you can, but adjust according to how well you are learning your specialty. If it sacrifices your understanding of your niche, then don't worry about extending it by a little. It's not going to be the end of the world if you come out of the other end as a master in your niche.

Finally, the most important part is to consider how this affects you as an influencer. Based on your understanding of the markets, what is the best way to utilize your new skills with your influence in a way that can make you your most effective self and can accelerate your business's success? You already know how to promote a business; it's just now the business you'll be working for is your own. On a side note about mentality, this can be both exciting and terrifying if you consider it. Your own business needs you to promote it and be the influencer for your own brand. Use your skills and make it your own. This step to authority is full of new opportunities to show off your abilities.

The influencer has many ways he or she can promote his or her business and make his or her newly founded authority evident.

Expert to Authority

The factors that make up the experts and influencers are not necessarily bad characteristics. Later, you'll see how an authority does end up dabbling in mastering his or her niche and has to remain consistent. He or she also has to gain experience and should definitely work to broaden his or her knowledge, but the key features below are what makes a great influencer or expert and make him or her the best version of him or herself that he or she can be.

As an expert, your process of progressing to an authority status will include increasing your ability to promote your skills and broaden your influence.

1. In what ways can you expand your promotional capacity? Look at how you are currently promoting your business to see what elements from the influencer side of the equation you could do more to develop.

2. How much can your current skills do for you? In other words, are your current skills sufficient, or do you need to expand your skill set? The answer to this one might come over time, but as long as you are able to consistently expand your business, this question shouldn't be too difficult to answer.

3. In what ways can you use your skills to augment your newly acquired influence? If you have already worked hard to gain valuable skills, then you should be able to promote them fairly easily. Just make sure that the skills are in and of themselves their own marketing tools (highly in demand, highly profitable, highly specialized).

When considering how you might expand your promotions and influence as an expert, the most effective way to look at it is if your skills are up to where they need to be, then you don't need to oversell them. What looks better, in the long run, is an active presence among your network and peers. If you have a strongly marketable skill set, as the last question asks, then you should have no trouble making your business highly influential in your niche. The core piece of your business model is the quality of your skills. After that, it's how you utilize those skills. For the sake of this book, we're mostly looking at past product development, past business model design, and looking instead at who we want to be. Do we want to be the average salesperson or above-average authority?

What skills will you be promoting for your business? Will it be something you know well? If so, then good, you're one step closer. The problem comes when you simply try to work that one skill to death instead of taking advantage of the books you could write on the subject, videos and courses you could be developing, and speaking that you could be doing. Granted, it is difficult for an expert to see more than wage services, to begin with. Part of it may have to do with years of experience or the common misconception that you have to be clocking in and out for your pay. The opportunities that being an authority affords range from high-profile seminars to workshops to online training camps. Maybe with a little ingenuity, you can genuinely produce deep content that can help everyone understand your skill set and unique craft just a bit better.

Never lower your target. Increase your action.

—GRANT CARDONE

CHAPTER 8

How to Become an Authority

U p to this point, we have discussed the elements of expertise and influence. Now, it is time to put it all together. You want to become an authority. You want your work to contribute value and uplift people. By this point, I hope you have at least become aware of things in your life that are holding you back, limiting beliefs that you need to let go of, and the direction you want to take in your life. Now you are ready to take the practical path to become an authority. The first step is easy. You have to pick the industry that you want to enter.

Fill the Void

Focus on one niche. You don't want to be a jack of all trades and master of none. If you look at any industry, you can find a void to fill. For me, when I was working for Paul, he had billions in business. His systems were good but he lacked in the social media and PR departments. That's the only thing I focused on because I knew that if I could do that, he would be good. I didn't worry about helping him with the other aspects of business; I wanted to provide extreme value in one particular need. Once I determined to do PR, I had to find a way to stick out in a crowded market. For PR, the industry has been run in a traditional way. People pay a monthly retainer, and there are no guarantees on the services. I realized that I needed to make my "shtick" guaranteed PR. Traditional companies would charge you five grand and turn around and tell you, "We will do our best to pitch you to networks and get you published." To me, that was absurd. It made me think of packing my bags, buying a ticket, and getting on the plane, but when you get on the plane, the pilot tells you, "Sorry, we aren't flying today." So I determined to break that model. I got a lot of backlash from different people in the industry, but that was my niche—guaranteed PR. This model has worked for me. I have published somewhere between five thousand to eight thousand articles. Traditionally, agencies would have to pitch one hundred thousand times to achieve those numbers. I don't have to do that.

Do It for Free

At the end of the day, people are pretty selfish by nature. We were created to be survivors. So when you are looking to find your niche, there has to be tangible value for the client. Back in 2018, I came up with an idea. I did research on the top twenty CBD companies that were around. I did an article called "Top 20 CBD

Companies in 2018," and I contacted all twenty companies and told them what I was working with. I gathered all the research and had them send me a lot of free samples. I ended up getting ten companies to say yes, and none of them paid me. Within a month of publishing the article (for free), I had six of those companies on retainer paying a minimum of $5K a month for a year. That's $30K for about three hours of my time. One of the companies took it one step further. The CEO called me and told me that "We love what you do so much that we will pay you a premium to not work with the competition." They offered me a bunch of stock options and paid me close to a quarter-million dollars a year. I accepted. At age twenty-five, I became the youngest C-level executive and was flying out to meet people like Ice Cube and other celebrities to help them get PR. Now, I know the free flights and the $250K/year were the things that stood out, but that's not the point of this story. The important thing is that I did this all for *free*. I addressed the naturally greedy nature of people and used it to leverage my way into a lucrative deal. As an authority, it is important that you make sure to meet others' needs before you look to meet your own. After that, you are able to start charging what you want but not until you have been recognized by others for your work.

Master Your Craft and Be Everywhere

Equally important is to be consistent and be everywhere. You're engaging in a critically important process, and it's one you cannot afford to treat like a side hustle. If that has been your hope for this process, to make it something you just do on the side, then let me correct that notion right here and now before we progress. You need to be engaged and present if you hope to be impactful. There is no easy road to authority or cheat code or hack to get you there. You have to make sure you are there, where it is all happening, to learn, engage, and connect. Your niche or the niche your business is in most likely has conferences, seminars, or functions you can attend. Whether it's mixers, conferences, or whatever kind of function it is, get there and get connected with like-minded people.

I know we live in the digital age, where we're all protected by our monitors and keyboards. It may be easy to think that's how you'll engage with people and how you'll become impactful. Just start posting, dial up the hashtags, boost the posts, and go, but that is only going to keep you at an influencer level. People need to meet you, get to know you, and trust you, and you need to meet them; you need to learn the names of people and get their contacts. Aim to connect and grow that inner circle of influence that will come to serve you well.

Attend all the conferences you can. While attending these conferences, connect with people to find your tribe and stay in touch with them. There are great speakers and leaders at these conferences too. Connect with these people and learn how they made it to where they are. You'd be surprised at what kinds of things you can learn from the examples of your network. Study those in your niche and genuinely connect with them as a peer. Use the conference environment as a medium for growth in your niche. You never know who is going to be the next big success, so treat your connections as important figures in your life. Give them the attention and respect they deserve, and they will, in turn, come to know you as someone they can trust. You may not be in their network now, but that can be easily changed with enough familiarity. Ultimately, become familiar with the people in your niche and give your inner circle every chance it needs to grow. Then keep contact with that network, and you'll find yourself in many situations where that network will have your back in the long run. Make sure you're present and taking care of your network, and they'll take care of you.

Self-Improvement

Continually improve yourself and learn your topic. Your education will be a continuous thing, so make it a priority for you now instead of waiting until you have to call in favors for the simple things in your niche. You will find that if you expand your knowledge in your niche, as we discussed earlier, you'll grow in confidence and performance. There are so many benefits to making your education a never-ending commitment. Never stop learning. Pay for courses, attend seminars and lectures, and take all of the opportunities for education that you can. The internet is full of content that can help you grow.

Keep current on that topic that you specialize in, including the latest best practices for influencers in that field.

How are they monetizing?

How are they engaging?

What kind of topics are hot in that field?

These are all valid questions that you might ask to gauge how the current climate of that niche is. Whatever you feel is working that field, heavily research it, then test it out as you roll new content out. The industries of today are experiencing such drastic changes that if you stay out of the loop for even a short period of time, you could find yourself completely behind the curve.

If there is one thing that I can tell you to do that you should keep, it's to stay current. There's nothing worse than seeing a recent post with outdated information, and your followers/readers will recognize that inconsistency much quicker than you think they will. The consumer of today is intelligent and has access to fact-checking, trends on social media, and every media outlet you have access to. So if you fall behind or make outdated claims or post things that are out of touch, you're going to invite backlash much stronger than in the past. It's an ever-changing market, and there's not much room for claims that you can't back up. Your goal should be honest posting, but honest, in-touch posting is even better if you do it well.

There's also a need to engage in a quickly changing follower base. Your followers on social media and in newsletters and emails will be closely attuned to the trends of the day and will notice if you're out of touch. It's not just what's trending, though. You also need to make sure that the information you are providing your audience is accurate and representative of the followers you have. If you're giving tips on marketing, make sure your statistics, advice, all of it, is accurate and from reliable sources. If you want a deeper engagement with your clients and followers, know the needs of the people and the businesses you are serving.

Keep growing and learning, and you are sure to satisfy the needs of those in your network and those that follow your business or brand. By satisfying the needs they have, you'll become their go-to when they need help in that niche. Knowing your niche is an invaluable trait that will help you to fill these needs within your circles. You'll become that authority they consult with over everything within your niche. Mastery is one of your strongest tools in achieving authority; use it well.

Collaboration/Brand Association

Collaboration is one of the greatest ways to expand your network and solidify your relationship with those in your network. If you are featuring other brands, linking other creators, or referring other businesses, you are collaborating. Maybe you're a freelancer, and you're bringing in your network to help with projects. That's you collaborating with your peers. People trust someone they've done work with if they like his or her work ethic, and if his or her work ethic speaks well about him or her, then those that have collaborated with him or her will have nothing but good things to say when asked about his or her performance in a certain niche or topic. A vote of confidence and character reference will always stand out over any other kind of method of recognition.

Collaborate on everything that you can. Reach out and ask if others in your inner circle are interested in a collaboration effort. In fact, go a step further and cold call for collaboration. Cold calling can be called "cold DMing" in today's terms. Message, email, elevator pitch—there are all kinds of ways to connect. The only reason you wouldn't connect is that you didn't make enough calls. Make it your elevator pitch when connecting with a potential long-term member of your network.

Make sure you use collaborations to show your skills and emphasize the skills of those you are collaborating with. If you are interviewing someone on your podcast, for example, then talk to them about subjects that allow them to promote projects they're working on. Treat their business, brand, and project as important as you would your own, and people are most likely to positively reciprocate. Concisely said, don't take the limelight when collaborating. Pass the mic and step back. In the above scenario, you're on your own podcast, and those who want to follow you have already done so. When doing a collaborative action in your life, showcase the great work of your peers. If you do it this way, you're collaborating right.

Working with another influencer at or above your level should be mutually beneficial. It can allow you to see his or her process and the things that have, in fact, made him or her the authority YouTuber in the room. If you want to learn how to be like someone, you have to first understand how he or she feels. You want to learn the mentality of a mentor in the niche that you're going to be in. If you can learn about how he or she achieved massive success on that platform in that sphere, then you can replicate it. Look for opportunities to work with someone who is more experienced than you in your niche so that you can grow into a stronger authority.

In the world of social media, the more advanced influencer is able to pipeline consumers to the smaller account's services and is able to grow him or herself. Learn from these successful influencers and collaborate with them. You'll find that new techniques of marketing are developed every day. You can continuously learn new techniques and ways to market in your niche. The only thing this growth requires is the self-education necessary to acquire new skills you can use in your business.

People look highly on someone who takes his or her time to help his or her fellow business owner and doesn't just rush his or her way through to the top, where he or she keeps it for him or herself.

The ability to collaborate also signals your ability to play well with a team and can become a reference for you in and of itself.

Put in the Work

Do the work. Do everything that is necessary and beware of cutting corners along the way. Success doesn't come overnight; this is true even for bloggers. Reject the "get traffic to get rich quick" schemes and put effort into your content, marketing, promotions, and networking. You're going to find those schemes take up just as much time as doing it right. In all honesty, they end up costing you more in the long run.

Give Credit

Publicly credit your inspiration. Suppose you get a chance to meet a high-profile figure, post about it, and tell about how he or she inspired you. Make sure that people understand the impact they had on your life. This also applies to those who are not as high profile. When you are inspired, go ahead and let that influencer know by tagging on social media and thanking him or her. Even if it legally is not his or her material, but he or she had a part in the inspiration, credit him or her. After your collaborations, give credit to the other participant; don't just take all of the credit.

Don't make it about yourself. Don't keep the credit when it's due elsewhere; there's nothing more damaging to your credibility. This doesn't mean you need to downplay your influence, but also don't embellish it at the expense of those who help create it with you. Not only does this take away from your respectability among your followers, but it also takes away from opportunities to collaborate with those other professionals in the future. You're trying to nourish relationships, not strike out on your own like a lone wolf. You want to work to stay close to a network of like-minded people, not work to alienate them. Keeping it about your niche community and your peers keeps you from alienating some of the most powerful assets you will ever have.

Create relationships with these owners who will be fruitful later on. If you have a quality network, you are saving yourself headaches and frustrations later on in your career. As a business owner, I have found the relationships you create early on last long after your business seemingly no longer needs that contact or brand that you've collaborated with. This flies in the face of the current model most experts or influencers form. Instead of shallow "follow for follow" hashtags and job boards for gig work, creating relationships is where the truest growth starts. Neither category is going to develop close relationships with clients if all they do is type back and forth with you or hire you for a job or endorsement, only to never speak with you again. What you're doing here is transcending the idea that you must have a large social media following to gather a reputation in your niche. This simply isn't true. Foster the relationship with your clients, and the income will come in. Be relationally focused, not necessarily follow focused.

Be Available

Be available. This is a simple one. It doesn't sound complicated when you think about it, but be available to be reached by clients, people in your inner circle, all of them. You need to make sure your availability can be on when you need it to be. If this means emails, clearing your calendar for talks and appearances, or whatever the process may look like for you, just make sure that if needed, you can be there. Make yourself available, and don't miss out on the opportunities to serve your clients.

Availability also means keeping yourself in a position to change your schedule if necessary. The goals of this step are to show that you are dedicated to your craft and to gain the most opportunities as possible to keep yourself close to the chances for professional growth. In short, keep yourself in a place where you can increase your own luck.

Be Creative

Online options for being present are a great way to connect. Whether it's a live Q and A on Facebook, YouTube, TikTok, or any number of apps, or a live stream through a streaming service, it can be interviewed on Spotify, local news websites, or even regular updates on your social media accounts through stories, reels, videos, and so on. The methods are virtually endless, but what's important is being visible to your followers. Stay visible, and don't drop off the radar. Doing this ensures your being considered a valid and influential figure in your circle.

Offline appearances are also incredibly important in expanding your influence. There are traditional options like book signings, meet and greets, and speaking at events, but that is hardly an exhaustive list of all the ways you can be present in an offline setting. An offline method coupled with an online medium can produce great results. For example, by coordinating your posts and appearances, you can simultaneously be live-streaming a talk you're giving and make yourself visible in both settings. The rule of thumb is the more visible you are, the better.

Diversify your content. If you're posting a lot of content over periods of time, you need to ensure that you're differentiating it. People get tired of the same old format and will engage with your page more if you have a variety. You should always be looking to make your content fresh and actively meet the different demographics of your clients. The good news is that there are many different kinds of content you can post for people to see and interact with. Depending on the platform, you have video, infographics, long-form articles, and social media. This will show you what works and help you crop up everywhere.

Speak at new, small venues in your niche. Use Blab, Facebook Live, or Periscope to build your speaking skills and portfolio and select smaller venues in newer up-and-coming settings or companies. You could try from day one to tackle speaking engagements at large venues with a huge company, but you're much more likely to leave an impact and be remembered, even to get a speaking engagement period, if you focus on small settings in newer venues. Following an old rule that competition is never as good as differentiation, the more diversified your approach is and the more approachable settings you utilize, the greater chance of leaving an impact you'll have.

Improve your reach. The practice of trying to promote site traffic is not relevant anymore. As an authority, you won't be sitting back passively waiting for someone to come view your page. You're going to find that, instead, proactively engaging your clients is a much better option. Forget page views if you want your influence to grow and instead focus on growing and engaging followers via social media and email subscribers. This last step in part 1 is all about creating a voice for yourself and expanding the notoriety you already have. The numbers show that social media is the best place to do this. Having the previous steps completed in their entirety is going to make this step the most effective version of itself. If you need to, go back and check off the previous steps prior to attempting to expand your influence.

Analyze your followers to optimize your posts' performance. To understand what the people viewing your content on a daily basis want to see, you'll need to treat this part as a simple market analysis to see what kind of content is making the biggest impact.

Focus on that content and make it a bigger part of your business model. If there are revisions you can make to the other areas of your courses or your content, then make the necessary changes, but learn to identify the portions of your services that are working best for you and make optimal use of those elements. Grow your following here, and you'll see exponential growth in the long run.

To best understand the needs of your clients, numbers can help you better than anything else. There are many online tools you can use to get a better understanding of what your client base needs or wants to see. Using survey services or questionnaires can help you gauge the opinions of your followers so that you can adjust your services to meet their needs. This doesn't necessarily mean you have to make any massive changes, just that your followers matter enough for you to make the necessary changes to help them where they actually need it. Adjusting and pivoting to where your clients need your help the most can go a long way in

These steps will take you into the pros and will give you an impact on your niche. The order you complete them in, while crucial, can be subject to change. For example, if you've come to find that your followers are leaning more toward one kind of occupation, you can take advantage of that information and ensure that you adjust your speaking engagements and courses to cater to that kind of occupation. Then you can look and see why you aren't quite as relevant with other occupations and what you can do to change your standing with them. The importance here is that you need to expand if you can, as that is how your business and authority will survive.

Information is useless if it is not applied to something important or if you will forget it before you have a chance to apply it.

—TIM FERRIS

Nurturing Your Peers and Followers

Maintaining a skill is just as crucial and often as difficult as gaining it. In this second part of learning how to become an authority, you'll learn how to take the authority you have already gained and maintain your position. You've followed the steps in part 1, now the hard part—maintaining your status. This section involves a lot of empathy and introspection. You'll need to take inventory of the different skill sets the other people in your niche already have and see how you can help them gain momentum. This involves teaching, advising, and looking for opportunities to create value for other creators around you. This nurturing process is how you can go from building your own career up to elevating those around you too.

This part will also have a heavy emphasis on service. You'll find in the coming years that your customers/clients really appreciate a service-driven focus. This kind of mentality illustrates you know your niche well enough to provide a needed product or service. Understanding your niche results allows you to target those who need your goods/services the most. Never forget to show appreciation to your customer and provide outstanding service, and you'll acquire a loyal, targeted audience.

I have not seen a person gain authority and simply remain stagnant, with no plans of paying it back. One prime example that comes to mind is Tony Robbins. Though you probably know him as the energetic, motivational speaker with a huge presence and years in the game, you may not know a side of him that has raised millions for the organization Feeding America.

Out of his own net worth, Robbins has matched contributions in the past and has generously donated to the organization. He also started the Tony Robbins foundation back in 1991 with the goal of transforming the lives of convicts, elderly people, addicts, the homeless, and many more. The presence he brings to the stage and through his several books is unique and highly influential. He could've stopped there and said that he was only doing this for himself. Instead, he saw an opportunity to make a difference using little more than the assets that were available to him and his influence. His authority in his niche benefited the lives of millions of people and continues to do so today. Robbins has used his authority to captivate audiences, motivate people to better themselves, push businesses to new heights, and yet among all of that, he has taken large amounts of his own capital and his time and dedicated it to those he knows who he, at some point, could've been just like. This shows the humility that exists in someone with authority because he sees that he was only decisions away from being in unfortunate situations. This humility shows itself in a willingness to go and make life better for the less fortunate and not just settle for enjoying the affluence that comes with an authority-driven life.

There's no reason you can't also find a way to contribute and help those in your community. That should be the goal of any person of influence and authority is to help make life better for those who are working toward the same goals as them. Making your authority work for your community is a great way to grow and give back to the individuals who have given to your business.

This chapter is primarily about maintaining the authority that you've worked hard to establish, but it's uncanny how so many times the right thing to do is what will take your authority and solidify it. A person of authority doesn't have to sacrifice his neighbor to be successful. That is something that you should be able to progress past.

Give Back to Your Peers

Give compassionate advice to your peers. Do your best to take the chances you get to speak to up-and-coming entrepreneurs in the same way you wish someone had spoken to you back when you were first starting. The point of these steps is to establish authority, and that's best done in a way that isn't pushy or demeaning. Help your peers by answering the questions they may have and do it in a generous way to get the best reception.

I've talked about my experiences with my mentor and how that gave me the edge I needed to create a successful career for myself. That would not have happened in that timing, maybe even at all, if my boss had not been more than a boss and had not decided to become a mentor. After receiving the training that I had needed the whole time, the trajectory of my life drastically changed and was far removed from the original course that it had taken. I always knew what I had wanted, and I knew how I would pursue it, but I didn't know I was lacking the necessary approach. The struggle of every person wanting to break out and start his or her path on his or her own is that he or she often wastes valuable years on the wrong methods and ends up frustrated. This is likely due to a lack of information or good mentorship and coaching. That's not a future you or I would wish on anyone, and it's one that he or she definitely doesn't have to experience. You can help people find their own authority by mentoring them. At the same time, you end up adding to your network and developing relationships with like-minded, driven individuals who are also looking to make a difference.

Speak from experience without being pushy. Don't let the pressure be too assertive to catch you off guard. Remember that confidence is quiet and calm. When you approach your peers, remember that everyone has different levels of expertise. If you want to impact them, keep in mind your expertise and their unique character. Talk to them through your experience to show what has worked in your career. It's possible that the way it worked for you might not work in their niche and understanding that will help you to come across as more caring and considerate than judgmental. Approach them with your experience, and they will appreciate the advice you have to offer.

Help New Players in the Game

Help the bloggers and other specialists behind you. Help the people who are two or three steps behind where you are today. Do you know someone up and coming in your niche? Don't just tag and feature him or her; pass him or her opportunities you can't accept so that he or she can have a chance at high-yield opportunities. Throw your peers and those you are mentoring some lifelines when possible, and you'll be surprised how much that will come back to benefit you later.

If you remember back to my beginnings, my whole career opened up because of one boss who not only mentored me but also gave me the chance to practice what he taught me. You can impact so many lives by giving motivated self-starters like yourself the chance to take on high-profile clients needing help completing projects. The problem most beginners face is the initial process of gaining momentum and forming a clientele.

Keep the Client First

Make serving others your mission. Once you've found your ideal customer, make everything you do about serving them. This mentality will take you from simply selling a product to designing a system that makes the product work for the customer. The purpose of service is to provide a satisfactory experience. Once you've established your authority, show your understanding of your niche by making it work for your customer. Don't cut corners and cheapen the process simply to drive your sales. That approach is one of the quickest ways to eliminate all of the work you've put into becoming an authority and going back to being just another profit-driven company. Don't lose the tribe you've formed, and don't sacrifice your authority for anything that could lower your standards.

If this principle becomes a cornerstone of your business practice, it will begin to show in how you operate your services. The services you operate can either be based on service or profit. If you focus on service, the profits will come, but if you model them around profit, you will definitely miss out on the service through them. There's no way you can optimally serve your community in a model that is nothing more than profit-driven.

1.   Create webinars. These are great opportunities to share your expertise and build a following. I've found webinars to be far superior to large documents, web pages, or pdf downloadables. If you give a visual aid like a webinar, then you'll find that you're much more likely to have people view it and recommend it. These webinars can be created at no cost. It doesn't matter so much as long as they contain vital content that contributes to the growth of someone's knowledge in your specific niche.

Webinars are perfect opportunities to promote premium content while still helping those who may need a full, in-depth program. By providing free content in the webinar, as an example, you can show your clients what to expect from a course or certain service you are offering. If they see the content upfront and know that they want to gain access to a deeper learning session with more information, then they pay and get the premium subscription.

Another note on webinars, they are an amazing way to figure out how you would like to further promote yourself and your product. Many people I know are concerned about public speaking and worry about how they sound in front of a crowd. The thing about a webinar is that it takes away that fear because you can't really see all of the people viewing your video. You know they'll be seeing it, but it doesn't really register the same way standing in front of a ton of people does. So you can practice and edit it how you like it. Then you can progress to public speaking arrangements. Live webinars are becoming the norm for many seminars that used to be done in person, largely due to the pandemic, so this can also be a way to start developing your speaking capabilities. For many, remote webinars are going to be an option for years to come. Taking advantage of the great asset a good webinar can be is a great way to utilize your authority even further.

Be Selfless

Now I know this sounds like the previous point, but you need to understand the difference. You can put your clients first but still be selfish. The truth is being a good person and having awesome customer service coupled with a good product or service will make you really good money, and people know that. So they build systems and businesses that cater to their customers, but their heart really isn't in it. When you are selfless, it's a little different. Creating a selfless model of running a business takes a customer-centric approach. What does this look like? Promotions, giveaways, services for the customer, and services designed to make the customer know that they are important. Not every action should be for pay or consideration. If you have talks and webinars that offer information for free, that is selfless service. That is a service that acts according to its mission of service.

Again, the model that works the best is one that is driven by service and selflessness and generates profit as a side effect. With any other approach, you lose your selflessness. A selfish model is something that is used when you are concerned that your business model and skill set are not enough to generate profit on their own. This insecurity is something that shouldn't be a concern for you if you're operating as an authority. As an authority, your profit model is already well secured in your ability to generate profit from your knowledge of a subject and the content that comes with that knowledge. You should be past the insecurity of profit and be able to consider the needs of those who are supplying your business with profit by consuming the content that you are producing.

Take the time to help someone in need instead of seeing every customer as a source of quick revenue or number on a list of followers. Use the resources your business has to make exceptions for customers; be ready with refunds and don't treat your customers like sources of revenue. Treat them with value, and I promise, you'll see it reciprocated.

There are so many people out there with amazing ideas and plans but no idea how to implement them. Now that you've learned how to share it with them, what does a selfless authority look like? It doesn't look like a bully who takes his or her success and flaunts it. It certainly does not look like a grifter who charges prices that are ridiculous and then offers less than quality content or services in return. Selflessness in this context looks like knowing that your business or brand is your opportunity to make a positive change in the world. Selfless authority doesn't have to belittle or take advantage to be profitable or successful. All it takes is an effective business plan and the heart to do the right thing by your peers. Take the selfless approach to your business, and you'll see the difference in response from your clients.

Stand Up for the Injustices in Your Niche

Do you see one of the little guys being crushed by a big organization? Stand up for their brand and promote them in your media. Point out the things that are being done to them and utilize your influence to help them. Is there a fellow blogger being unfairly smeared? Stand by them, and don't worry if you polarize a few customers. Remember that cooperation is key and that same business is part of a major community that you've joined. Did you find stolen content that belongs to someone else? Speak up and help your fellow man. Don't allow content theft on your site, and don't allow it to go unnoticed. Be the difference in the community. Even if you are in direct competition with the company being wronged, it does nothing for your brand name and your position of authority to help them fail. You're indirectly fighting for your own brand when you fight for the brand or company in your circle that is being wronged—standing up for the other brands in your niche, while the right thing to do, will also be seen as a sign that your business practices are trustworthy and put people first.

Putting your principles first is never the wrong move, especially when your name is associated with your brand and the values that are represented by that brand name. Taking action to keep people taken care of and keep your tribe safe is the surest way to develop lasting loyalty.

In conclusion, as an authority, your brand needs to be closely tied to your ultimate goal. Commit to advocacy in your niche. If there's an ethical matter that is being violated, don't allow yourself to become part of the problem. There are many stances you can take as an individual, but as an authority figure, try to see the big picture before you make public statements about what all is happening in the world. You want to be not only factually correct but also remain relevant too.

Use your platform to champion causes that otherwise might have gone unnoticed. If there's a cause that you can contribute to through your work, then contribute. Make it a priority for your business to feature that cause in your materials and fund them whenever possible. If there are opportunities to help educate and coach people from backgrounds that leave them at a disadvantage, then commit to helping that person reach the potential that he or she previously thought wasn't possible. Mentor those around you and offer help wherever necessary. Spread the word about a cause. As an authority, the causes you support stand to greatly benefit. Find one that you are passionate about and make it a major part of your business. Collecting signatures, sharing petitions, and making calls are just a few of the ways that you can make a difference for a cause or charity. Utilizing your business influence will go a long way to making you an effective advocate and authority. It is also worth remembering that while you may not feel like it's acceptable to use charity work in marketing material, there is nothing wrong with showcasing your businesses pursuit of

Your authority can be solidified by these simple steps. The process does involve some actions that many businesses and people don't take, but that's why I emphasize them here. It's about separating yourself from others and standing out as a unique authority figure. You can try and be better at competing with others, or you can make yourself stand out.

There is no need to compete as an authority. You can bypass the job boards, the small handouts of payment for your services, and can set your own price. Along the way, you can build your business the way you see fit. You can offer free services and help those you meet. You can become a stronger force for good. With sufficient authority, you can step outside of the competitive rat race and enjoy a solid network of peers and clients who will supply you with enough work to keep you busy.

If you follow these steps, maybe even starting today, you are guaranteed to see drastic changes in your authority. Don't be in too much of a rush. I can promise that at first glance, the process seems to take too long, while in reality, the results quickly begin to come.

The question then becomes, now, with your authority established, how do you make it work for you? How will you go and monetize the expertise that you have, the influence that you have? How can all of that work for you and your unique profile of experiences and skills?

Don't find fault, find a remedy.

–TONY ROBBIN

CHAPTER 10

Monetizing Authority

The results of being an authority present are endless. It can create interest in your services and the causes you fight for. Once you've established it, you have the ability to make changes and influence people you never thought you'd ever meet before, but when it comes to monetizing authority, the picture seems to get a little fuzzy for some. To make the most out of your authority, you'll need to have a strategy for monetizing it. While some of the methods I'll show you may be self-explanatory, I have a few options here that I imagine you didn't think were things that someone could just one day start doing and making money.

The authority has the best parts of the influencer and the expert. They have specialized their skills but are not restricted to a core set of clients. Their definition of who they can serve is much broader than that, and they remain flexible in case they need to pivot at a later date. This can create an easier plan of monetization as the specific set of clients are only a portion of the population they can provide services for. The greatest assets of the authority are their ability to monetize and grow in a way that both the influencer and the expert struggle to do. The intersection between these two specialties is where the authority finds their workflow and where they can act according to their true potential.

The authority's ultimate pursuit is infinitude. Whether it's within their network or niche, the authority should be able to achieve a position where they no longer have to slave to keep updating themselves on a yearly basis. The purpose of this book is to solidify infinitude and keep the authority that they have achieved active for years to come. Monetizing that authority and putting it to work is one great way to achieve this. By using your authority, you can come to understand the effect you have on your specialty and in your circles. An effective monetization plan is also an effective maintenance plan.

Monetizing Your Specialty

Gaining authority gives you a strong position to monetize your specialty. Depending on the niche market you're serving, this can look like different things. If you're a graphic designer, this can look like simply getting paid to design projects for clients. The difference for this initial category is that when you were working to monetize your specialty as an expert, you lack the broad influence to reach high-profile clients and big-ticket projects. There's a difference between designing a project that you spent days pursuing as a potential client and designing a project for a client that looked you up, contacted you, and asked you to design for them.

Monetizing your specialty becomes much easier when you have the social proof and broad network to speak for you. The process becomes much simpler, and you spend less time making calls, sending proposals, providing a CV, and trying like crazy to get some work. Let's go back to the example of the graphic designer who has gone from small-time clients that he or she pursued on a job board to high-profile firms who came to him or her instead. This designer now has the ability to take their pick of the jobs that he or she wants instead of having to settle for gigs that won't pay what his or her work is really worth. He or she has gone above the point of taking the jobs he or she can land and is now choosing projects based on what works best in his or her schedule and achieving the goals that he or she has set for him or herself. This is just one of the ways a great network can work for you by connecting you with options for work that fit within your specialty.

The use of your authority has its applications in gaining higher returns for things that you may have been underpaid for before. I've mentioned how I want to see both influencers and experts getting the recognition they deserve, and I do mean that. I hope that through the monetization of your skill set, you'll be able to see returns that are much greater than the ones you enjoyed before. The point is to radically increase your returns in a category of work that you enjoy doing. The only way of obtaining that goal is to pursue the work that you're passionate about with authority, utilizing your authority to promote that work to people who will pay you what you are worth. Most specialties I can think of have a way to monetize and tie in well with content ideas that you could develop into webinars, courses, or book material.

What has bothered me about our modern system of online business and wealth is that there is such a strong, central wealth accumulation that ultimately leaves the hard-working self-starters to only take percentages off the top and not receive the full pay that they deserve for their commitment and dedication. The influencer and the expert are underpaid. They're both underpaid by people who could never do the things that they do. Their specialty is used for another person's gains, and they are left with little to show for it.

Maybe you've noticed in your own career how those who drum up the most business are the ones least paid by the company. Or maybe you've noticed that those who do the footwork, in the case of experts, are the ones who enjoy the worst returns and that the executives don't care. They would rather take from you all of the work they can than pay you what you have earned. If you remain in this kind of situation, you could miss out on the work/

life balance that establishing yourself as an authority affords you. You can see how, after working my tail off for a multinational, billion-dollar fast-food chain, I was slightly resentful when I was only compensated with bare minimum wages. It doesn't have to be that way. The skilled and the influential do not have to get punished for the work that they excel at.

To achieve the monetization you have earned, gain expertise in your niche and learn how to be influential and impactful in your specialty. This should end up netting you the returns in terms of recognition for your authority but also in the form of pay, pay that you have earned on your own. Never be afraid to work for free, of course. You're not becoming some mercenary, but at the same time, know your work's worth. There are many times when you need to showcase your skills for a potential client, and that may require some work that will not be compensated. In the end, if you're leveraging your skills with authority, the issue compensation will not be one that you have too much trouble with. The point is to understand that the compensation for your services will come, and it will be adequate. You don't want to get caught up penny-pinching and charging for every single thing that you do. If you've created an environment where the work you are doing is something you are passionate about and love to spend your time doing, then the act of committing to some hours of work for free will not bother you. It will only allow you to feel freer to spend your time doing what makes you satisfied and fulfilled. Know what kind of work you are capable of delivering, and don't settle for returns that are drastically less than what you know you are able to make.

Monetizing by Consulting

A great way to monetize authority is to start consulting. As a consultant, the authority is not restricted to any specific clientele and is usually open to providing expertise on their specialty for whoever or whatever business may need it. As a consultant, you're getting paid to give your opinion and help create strategies for your clients. You're also getting paid to act as an educator and marketer at the same time. No matter the industry or time period, there seems to be a similar process. This structure can make it difficult to put an exact hour and time to the amount of time that a consultant works, but in the end, the payment model is relatively simple. Breaking into consulting may be the single most profitable monetization schedule for you as an authority.

A consulting authority is there to help the business grow, not just to rake in a profit. In many business models, consultants get a bad rap for showing up and simply inflating numbers as their business model. If you can truly add value to the company, then you should definitely try to. The more skills you have, the more people and businesses will take notice. I still advocate for being consistently great at one thing, but if you are already a person with many interests, I would encourage you to start out on your authority path as a consultant. This gives you the opportunity to monetize the skills you have and to add to the many other opportunities for monetary growth.

An authority consultant is a type of consultant who can articulate what he or she can do to fix a dilemma. The authority character speaks firmly but without judgment as to abstain from eliciting a defensive stance from those they attempt to help. They know it's hard to monetize a business and even more difficult to sustain one. Remember, it's not the type of business that is important when establishing authority. You don't want to be the third or fourth coffee shop on that street. You want to differentiate yourself or your business. If you're consulting, and your clients are the third or fourth coffee shop on the street, they are going to taste it to extend that metaphor. You want them to see and hear a different kind of voice in their offices that haven't been there before. This is why you don't operate with big buzzwords and flashy statements that are completely worthless.

No, you call them out on their mistakes, and you show them what they are doing wrong. This kind of honesty is rewarded in an ironic twist. Your integrity with them could be what keeps them from failure, and they will see that and reward it if you honestly approach them.

The process of monetizing being a consultant isn't just showing up and talking with business owners. It's much more than that. As a consultant, you'll be writing, speaking in public, appearing on podcasts, publishing articles, and discussing the practices and processes of the specialty that you are in on the news and websites. There are so many ways you can deliver revenue in this role that there is no real clear-cut way to define it, but if you break it down, these are some of the things that you would be doing as a consultant:

- Helping your clients solve the problems in their organization

    - Create plans and solutions for individual companies

- Showing them actively how to implement the fixes that you have prescribed for their business

    - Giving out plans for implementation and workflow practices that can help their workers accomplish their goals.

- Making a deal to stay on as a retainer to help while new processes are being implemented

    - This could look like a plan you offer that gives them access to you or an employee of yours who can answer quick questions he or she may have after implementing your plans

- Writing books on your processes and experiences

- ◻ Take your experiences and tips and write at least one book on them. You'd be surprised how many

- Creating a website/YouTube channel documenting your life and all that goes into your work

  - ◻ This is similar to the book idea but is more like a regular update of your progress, activities, and workflow. You can even give small tips of the trade along the way to encourage viewership.

- Developing a course on breaking into consulting

  - ◻ A course is an absolute must in the long run. You need to have a recorded course to receive repeat follower interaction and the ability to teach a broader audience about the purpose of authority.

- Give talks on the practices that you teach businesses with broader applications.

  - ◻ In-person talks are still a huge market, even with the internet being where almost everyone hosts their talks these days.

These are just a few of the ways you can capitalize on your experience and authority as a consultant. The beauty of this business model is that in helping the individuals or businesses who are your clients, you create content in the form of stories, examples, techniques, experience, and such. With that content, you can then turn around and use it to monetize even further. By the end, you are able to create a continuous series of writing, speaking, and creating where you are not just one specialty, but several, all working on the same niche.

Alternative Investment Opportunities

One of the biggest differences as an authority is the alternative investment opportunities you gain access to. When you think about "everyday" people, we don't have access to a lot of deals that others do. Yes, we can trade on the stock market, we can even get access to some IPOs and the ability to buy cryptocurrency, but that's all at the consumer level. By the time this is available for the everyday person, a crapload of money has already been made on these investments. The perfect example is a buddy of mine, Jeff Sekinger. I met Jeff back in 2018. We were speaking on stage together at the USC conference center in Los Angeles. We met each other and started chatting. It wasn't a long conversation. I shared what I was good at, and he shared what he was good at, and we parted ways. However, a year later, I was trying to find someone who was good at cryptocurrency because I wanted to invest some money in it. I knew there was some potential there, but I just didn't have the time to put into it. That's when I remembered Jeff. I hit him up, and we talked again. Very long story short, I invested money into his newly formed cryptocurrency fund, and

I made my money back and more in a short amount of time. This is just one simple example. Over the last few years, I have had many similar experiences like this. I bumped shoulders with someone who had an awesome opportunity because I was invited to speak at some event, join a mastermind, or something like that. These opportunities only came about because I was viewed as an authority and invited to these different kinds of events.

Go the extra mile, there's no one on it.

—GRANT CARDONE

CHAPTER 11

Maintaining and Expanding Your Authority

The process of achieving authority can open up opportunities you never had before. From this newly found position, you can expand and maintain your authority to make yourself even more impactful and effective. In expanding, you can reach people you never reached before and apply your skills to newer industries, where your business can change and grow.

Establishing anything, whether it's a company or habit, requires regular maintenance. You can't just start and expect it to roll on without any help, and you can't expect your followers and clients to continue to see your services as legitimate without a regular reminder of what you are all about. Your routine needs to be centered on the goal of generating value-driven content and products that can help your clients, expand your own understanding of your craft, and can ultimately result in a monetized asset. Your routine needs a creative space, a discipline-driven environment, and sufficient time to realign your goals when you feel that work has been too much. It's crucial to remain sustainable.

Practice in private to gain success in your business. As Tony Robbins states, "It's what you practice in private that you will be rewarded for in public." If you're molding your day around a maintained and purpose-driven routine, then your life and career are going to follow.

After establishing your authority, there are many steps you can take to maintain and expand it. You will need to focus on the following:

- The routine of an authority;
- The network of an authority;
- An authority's assets;
- Self-maintenance as an authority; and
- Continuous goals of an authority.

The Routine

Maintaining your authority is most effective when it becomes part of your regular routine. You should think of it as part of your day, the same as working out, making your bed, anything that you may have down to a routine thing. There are many entrepreneurs, influencers, and stars that make it big, gain authority, and lose it all because they become cocky and rest on their laurels. This process is supposed to be a lasting one, so it's only natural that you treat it like a lasting part of your life. It will follow you through all of the years you have worked in your specialty, and it will be a key characteristic in your success.

As a part of your journey, you are going to be creating routines and sticking to them to keep the success you've generated on a continuous basis. If you're fit and in great shape, you have to keep the habits going, or you'll quickly lose the shape you're in. If you are a great musician, you have to practice. If you are a hockey player, soccer player, or baseball player, you have to get out there and run drills. You have to practice and gain the daily edge you need to move your performance in the right direction.

Your routine is essential. You may wake up, wash your face, do a hundred pushups, and then go about your day. Or you may wake up, run a mile, and go about your day. Or, you may wake up, have some coffee, sit, watch the sunrise, and then go and crush your day. I think it is necessary to acknowledge that your process will be unique for you, and as long as it is unlocking your potential for progress, keep doing it. Don't lose yourself in all of the information out there about what constitutes the best daily routine or best work routine. You decide that for yourself. What I am most concerned with, in terms of a daily routine, is one that involves following your plan to gain authority and use it to its greatest extent. This looks like planning and implementing creative projects, speaking engagements, and online content that daily shows your followers that you are keeping up with your specialty and maintaining your influence.

Take my advice, we're all differently built, and we all find inspiration and motivation from different sources. I have my own set of icons and legends I look up to. Over the years, the stories from their lives have helped me grow my authority and understand my purpose better. This may be different for you. I am sure you have your own set of motivational individuals whose examples have driven you. As long as you are living up to the principles of authority, you will end up maintaining it however works best for you and your specific specialty. No two authority figures are built the same, and even if they were, their path to becoming an authority would still be different. It's important to drop the tendency we all have to compare ourselves with our peers and understand that success is defined differently. Aspire for your own goals, and use the authority you gain to reach them and make them the success you intended them to be. Don't get caught up in someone else's authority, the size and makeup of his or her network, or his or her ability to do something you might not be able to do. You're made of something he or she isn't and are perfectly capable of accomplishing your own success.

The network you create as an authority is one you will want to hold on to and expand as time goes by. A network is as good as the sum of the individuals that make it up, and each individual is a person with his or her own unique life and needs. Treat your network as a vital part of your authority that requires attention and maintenance. Your network is your legacy, and it's your best source of support at times

To keep that network, you'll find it's a good practice to keep in touch with them. Keep in contact with your network and find ways to collaborate with them. Find ways to keep in touch with them by making them part of your regular business. Develop a good network so you can form collaborations to plan speaking and networking events. Keep that inner circle close and stay in contact. They will often be your most reliable source of work and influence. If you are maintaining your network, you save time and energy by having a close source of industry information, work leads, potential clients, and source of information.

There are many ways to expand your network too. You will be attending all kinds of events already, based on the steps that establish your authority from earlier. If you are cultivating a strong network and don't have much time for a new contact just yet, make sure you get contact information from some of your peers that you meet at different events and keep them nearby until a later date, when you have been able to expand your schedule to accommodate a larger network.

There will come a point when your network is no longer sustainable if it continues to grow larger. We all only have twenty-four hours in a day, and there is a limit on how many people we can be communicating with all of the time. Take from your current network your highest-yield connections and focus on those connections. It's never ok to simply ghost a peer, but it's perfectly ok to cultivate your relationship with a higher profile member of your network if it means that you can gain notoriety. Use your connections and use them wisely. Don't abuse their contact information, and don't hesitate to slightly market within your group or network. You don't have to openly tell people that they need to be in your inner circle, but if you are able to, utilize your influence to show them that there is a benefit in being in your inner circle. Ensure it will remain sustainable, and you should have a fresh supply of influential people coming into your network.

As time goes on and your network expands, allow yourself the time and resources to keep in touch with valuable members. If you're leaving plans incomplete and meetups canceled, you're running the risk of alienating the circle of influence that you've worked so hard to construct. While it may run the risk of sounding like you're planning on using people, that is definitely not the case. You should be adding value to them and their businesses as time goes on. The key to maintaining a network is to give what you get. As your network expands, your impact expands too. You have the ability to affect more and more businesses and serve many more clients than before. Part of this process involves being an asset to those in your network, just like they're an asset to your business. In a way, this creates a relationship that thrives on reciprocating. As you help them over time, they help you too. Become a partner in business with your network, and they are sure to reciprocate when you need their help.

The Assets

The assets of authority are anything from the business assets owned to the knowledge and experience that the authority has accumulated over time. Without maintaining these assets, the authority will lose their ability to monetize over time and will not be able to serve their clients. The assets of an authority are what set them apart from others. They are the traits they rely on to remain calm under pressure and deliver results.

The most notable asset of an authority is their ability to apply their skills to solve the problems their peers are facing. By becoming an authority, you are essentially becoming a problem solver. Your primary job is to find out how you can solve the issues your network and clients are facing, and you are simply using your skills to do so. This skill is something the expert and the influencer cannot boast about. Their job is to find the

An authority's assets can also include their network. It's through your network that you'll find most of your most meaningful jobs will come. In your network, your inner circle will supply you with a lot of work, social proof, and opportunities to grow and expand. This network will be the circle that keeps you growing as an authority and will itself be an asset that you cannot ever afford to lose. Keep your network, keep them close, and expand them as time goes by.

The final asset of an authority is their ability to pass it on. The struggle to gain recognition and the work it takes to advance in your niche is a tough one. Many have given up on the way, and many more are two steps away from going back to mediocrity. The many business models that are thrown away somewhere probably had genius ideas behind them and simply poor execution. In this kind of world, the authority is able to take the success they are enjoying and pass it on to the next generation of authority figures.

The Self-Maintenance

Part of maintaining your authority is the practice of self-maintenance. This is a balanced process that needs a balanced individual to carry out. I'm advocating for your authority, but I want you to practice selflessness when dealing with customers and humility when working with your peers. In the same way, you need to keep moving your goals forward, but give yourself rewards and positive feedback along the way to keep your mind and body maintained. The last thing you want to do is burn out or become sloppy and careless with your business.

Self-maintenance requires discipline, discipline to keep track of your work, home life, network, and discipline to take care of your mind and body. Cultivating discipline will help you in the maintenance process, and as we've said, long-term maintenance is key. You have to remain disciplined in the process of building your character.

Creating the life you want looks like taking care of yourself too. There's no point in killing yourself at work if what you're working at isn't achieving what you want to achieve. I was burnt out and exhausted at my McDonald's job. I lost sleep because I would work late into the night on my business and wake up exhausted the next morning, still having to go to work and not able to take much time off at all. I was either in a hot, sweaty, fast-food kitchen or tired on my day off but having to work away at my business launch. To be honest, I don't regret all of that work, but it was coming from a place of not understanding how to be successful and become an authority. My time would have been much better spent had that business launch happened after I was mentored and understood the principles that I understand now.

As you know, my first attempt was a failure. I was grinding away at a business that soon after launching failed. Had I known what

I know now, I would've treated my life balance differently and worked harder on gaining insight into how to become an authority. Like so many people out there, I simply didn't know the secrets to unlock my own authority that I was able to learn later. The work I put in for my next business launch, while still challenging and exhausting, was more purposeful and directed correctly. If you're in my position, you may simply be trying to bridge the gap between struggle and performance, and that's usually a matter of technique and knowledge, not effort.

The next business launch of mine was a very different experience that resulted in my successfully growing my PR firm into a success. Once you know how to become an authority, the goal should become to create an environment where you can sustain momentum and work toward a stronger, more impactful career. The problem with most people grinding away all hours of the night is that many are working hard at something that isn't the best option for them and won't be as fruitful as it could be if they would operate with authority. I don't want to discourage you from hard work or chasing your dream, but the purpose of hard work should be to supply you with the life you want to live, and if you're too busy to live it, maybe you're doing something in a less-than-optimal way. Pace yourself and allow the process to take the time that it needs to take. You're on your own time and no one else's. Self-maintenance looks like self-discipline, but it also looks like taking care of yourself along the way. Maintain your work-life balance, authority, and growth by tackling and figuring out your version of self-maintenance early on, and you'll be able to stay in the game without dropping out. Keep yourself fresh for tomorrow, and don't lose sight of your ultimate goal of authority.

Continuous Goals

To maintain your authority, you need to keep your goals continuous. Updating your goals as you grow is crucial to maintaining your advantage in your niche. If you stagnate, slow down and settle, or start becoming complacent along the way, it will definitely show. It will cause you to make mistakes, get sloppy, and allow your hard-earned gains to regress. To keep your authority going, you need to never be satisfied with stopping.

Scanning your progress and keeping current with yourself is of the utmost importance. If you think back on the example I gave of our company expanding and eventually having to power ads back down to renew the quality of our services, you'll see that it's always a good idea to reassess your growth and reassess your potential. Doing so can give you the ability to catch opportunities as they come your way.

This continuous mindset is characteristic of every authority figure whose life I try to live and learn from. One such man is Grant Cardone. If you know about his story, you know that he went through rough times and became addicted to drugs at a young age. Cardone today runs a company with almost 2 billion worth of real estate in assets. However, his massive success hasn't been under just one line of work. In fact, the first job that put him on the map was a sales job at a car dealership, a far cry from a real estate empire. Cardone has written books, hosted and promoted massive events, spoken on several media networks, and has begun the Grant Cardone Foundation, a charity that provides mentoring for kids that have lost a parent. The list of his successes goes on, but the point is that he, at no point, allowed apathy to take over and instead focused on what was next and around the corner.

If you look back over the career that Cardone has led, you'll see several different hats being worn, sometimes at the same time, and several different, completely unrelated goals being worked toward. This isn't to say that he has a chaotic and unfocused style of working, far from it. He simply doesn't stop setting goals for himself. As a salesman, he made his goal to sell better than anyone he worked with and soon after became so good at it that he was training people in sales techniques. As an author, he set his goals to get his books written and published, and as a real estate investor, he set his goal to own a gigantic real estate portfolio. He has been successful in at least three major industries, completely disrupted automotive sales, and used his platform to accelerate the careers of thousands of like-minded people who simply want to achieve more in life. This was all possible because he did not settle and continued to pursue authority from early on in his career. Cardone chose to pursue his best possible self and made the most out of the career he began.

Each individual goal could have set him for life and have provided for him and his family, but Cardone describes himself as being easily bored and having an addictive personality that kept wanting to go further and further. It was establishing himself as an authority and not just remaining an expert salesman that allowed him that initial pivot from one role to an entirely new one. Cardone started a consulting company in the automotive industry as a way of establishing that authority, and soon after, he was on his way to starting company after company and expanding each to their fullest capacity. His career may have started when he became incredibly good at sales, but if you ask me, it wasn't until he decided that just excelling at sales and working in that capacity for the rest of his life wasn't going to be his legacy. His legacy was to become a career that has made him one of the most talked-about entrepreneurs in the world.

This is a great point to end on because as an authority, this is what the rest of your life will look like as long as you are working to remain an authority. You can keep working on one thing or twenty. It doesn't matter as long as you position yourself to be the one who chooses. If you don't take control and instead you let the markets decide for you, then you run the risk of putting yourself back in a position of losing out on your fullest potential. There's no doubt in my mind that the most successful people are those who carve out the discipline to maintain their success over the years of their lives. The difference in pros may only be a second, but the difference between short-term success and someone who enjoys authority for his or her whole life is a daily commitment to his or her goals and to him or herself.

You can take back your right to choose what kind of career you'll have, no matter what industry you are in or want to be in. The ability to make the kind of changes in your career that will accelerate your life is predicated on your ability to continuously place new goalposts in front of yourself and stay flexible with the growth you will experience. It all starts with the discomfort with mediocrity, and from there, it's just a matter of allowing that discomfort to drive you to pursue your infinite authority.

12

Time for Action

If you're reading this section, you've either skipped ahead, or you've taken a step that only a fraction of individuals have attempted. You've taken an honest look at yourself and seen where you can improve. At this point, the concept of infinite authority is second nature to you, and you're ready to put these topics into action.

I believe in the information I have shared in this book. However, *it's worthless without consistent action*! As much as I learned working under Paul, I would've stayed working for him or someone like him unless I took action. I had to take everything he had taught me and everything I had gathered from being around him and apply it to my own life. Once I did, the results were life-changing. The same applies to this book. You now understand the difference between an influencer and an expert. You know, understand the elements of influence, how to monetize your authority, and everything else, but until you take action, it means nothing. Now, you may not be ready to dive in gung-ho on your next venture, but the actions you start taking now need to point in that direction. I may sound biased, but I believe that everyone should invest in a mentor. As I said before, my time with Paul helped me to skip the bottom stairs of entrepreneurship, which ultimately saved me money and time. You can find a mentor locally, online, or invest in a solid program like my *Authority Accelerator,* which will take you through the steps to building a business and quickly establishing yourself as an authority in your field. I would love it if you chose my program. Whether you continue with my program, a mentor, or something else, the number one thing you can do is take the first step. Nothing can replace the action of stepping out of your comfort zone. Find something you are good at and figure out how it can make you money. Market it and start the process of becoming an authority. If you never read this book, followed me on social media, or took another piece of advice from me ever again, but you took the first step to change your life, I would be happy. I look forward to hearing the success story of every single last one of you who decides to take action and takes the first step toward gaining *Infinite Authority.*